For those who've wondered what the Peace Corps might be like, Jack Allison's narrative gives us a detailed and colorful first-hand account ... that not only demonstrates what Americans can do for the world, but also what that experience does to the volunteer.

— *James M. Dedman III*
Director of Academics, Retired
National District Attorneys Association
University of South Carolina

Jack Allison's book is a valuable contribution to the history of the Peace Corps in the 1960's and its presence in a recently decolonized part of Africa. More than that, though, it is a captivating and inspiring memoir by one of the Peace Corp's most remarkable volunteers, written with humor and a clear eye for irony. Combining his musical talents with deep compassion for his friends in Malawi, Jack spread his message of public health and human decency, often in the face of formidable personal and political obstacles. A warm heart at work in *The Warm Heart of Africa!*

— *Dr. John A. Hutcheson, Jr.* —
Professor of History, Emeritus
Dalton State College

President Kennedy inspired several generations to serve our country and the world. While some took up the charge in the armed forces, perhaps naively hoping to achieve some semblance of justice within the context of our numerous ongoing conflicts, Sargent Shriver led the way in regional development, public health, medicine, culture, and the pursuit of what might be called democratic infrastructure, internationally, with the Peace Corps, generally demonstrating along the way the inherent decency and kindness of the American people. Jack Allison signed up for the program, and this account of his life-altering work in Southeastern Africa makes for compelling reading. It's a page-turner I couldn't put down...

— *John W. Lambert* —
Co-Author, The North Carolina Symphony: A History, &
Editor in Chief, Classical Voice of North Carolina

The
Warm Heart
of
Africa

An Outrageous Adventure of
Love, Music, and Mishaps
in Malawi

Jack Allison

A PEACE CORPS WRITERS BOOK

The Warm Heart Of Africa
An Outrageous Adventure of
Love, Music, and Mishaps
in Malawi

A Peace Corps Writers Book – an imprint of Peace Corps Worldwide

For more information, contact peacecorpsworldwide@gmail.com.
Peace Corps Writers and the Peace Corps Writers colophon
are trademarks of PeaceCorpsWorldwide.org

Interior and Cover Design by:
Vally M. Sharpe
United Writers Press
Asheville, N.C.
www.UnitedWritersPress.com
828-505-1037

Unless otherwise noted, all photographs herein were
provided by the author and/or are in the public domain.

ISBN: 978-1-950444-10-6 (print edition)
ISBN: 978-1-950444-12-0 (eBook edition)
Library of Congress Control Number: 2020908301

First Peace Corps Writers Edition, May 2020

To Sue Wilson, my incredibly supportive wife—who is also my best friend;

To the memory of G. D. Chitowe-Phiri, my Peace Corps Malawian counterpart and dear, dear friend. Known by his patients as Dr. Nkanda, Achitowe died peacefully on May 9, 2020, at age 85.

&

The warm, welcoming, wonderful people of the country of Malawi.

To the memory of Judge Monroe G. McKay, my Peace Corps Director in Malawi.

To the memory of Andy Oerke, my Peace Corps Associate Director in Malawi.

To our children and their spouses: Adrienne & Bob; Josh & Olguita; Ginger; Tammy.

To our grandchildren: Nicole, Paul, Alex, Izzy, Nora, Zachary, & Xander.

And to our great grandchildren: Lili, Michael, Gabriel, & Jayden.

Contents

Contents

AUTHOR'S NOTE

The following names, listed in alphabetical order, are pseudonyms:

Ambrose, Beverly, Chad, C.R., Derek, Jill, Juanita, Judy, Junius, Loreen, Nate, Ned, Rhonda, Sam, Sheri, Ted, Vic, Zeb.

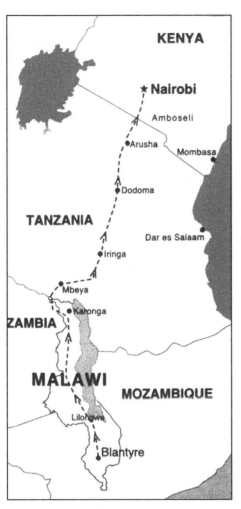

Malawi

Prelude

"Virtually every writer I know would rather be a musician."

Kurt Vonnegut

I wrote this book as a reflection of how my three years of service with the U.S. Peace Corps in Malawi, Central Africa, have had such a positive impact on my life and how the underlying substratum of music as a teaching medium has resulted in my unique approach to public health education.

Writing music was something I'd not done before going to Malawi, yet it ended up providing me with an enchanted, invaluable experience as a Peace Corps Volunteer. Many facets of living and working in Africa were different—language, customs, food, culture, conditions, comfort, communication, illnesses, transportation. The constants were friendship, acceptance, love, teaching and music.

In 1994, I visited Nsiyaludzu Village for the first time in twenty-five years. That place and the surrounding communities had been my home for three years. I was in Malawi that time by the invitation of Project Hope to help fight—with my music—the raging AIDS epidemic throughout the country.

That's when I first thought about writing a memoir to chronicle my experiences as a Peace Corps Volunteer, a public health educator who used music to deliver health-improving messages to the masses. It also chronicles my personal evolution from potential pastor to academic emergency physician.

It's taken another twenty-five years for this tome to be birthed.

The
Warm Heart
of
Africa

DAY ONE IN MY VILLAGE

"To me there is no picture so beautiful as smiling, bright-eyed, happy children; no music so sweet as their clear and ringing laughter."

P.T. Barnum

Leaving Blantyre, the commercial capital of Malawi, and where the Peace Corps office was located, the hundred-mile ride to Nsiyaludzu Village precipitated a spectrum of emotions in me: I was excited and a tad scared, yet full of hope and anticipation. Although I had worked hard and subsequently done well with the one-month immersion course in Chichewa in Puerto Rico, I also knew that I was barely facile with the basics of the language.

There were three of us in the cab of the Bedford lorry—Jere, the driver, John, a PCV headed farther up country for Kaphuka, and I. The truck was old, loud, hot and rough-riding—she bucked us thoroughly all the way. We two PCVs tried to converse in Chichewa with Jere, who spoke just a little English:

I started by asking, *"Jere, muli bwanji?"* [How are you?]

"Ndili bwino, kaya inu?" [I'm fine, how about you?]

"Ndili bwino'so. Zikomo kwambiri. [I'm fine, too. Thank you very much.]

John repeated the exchange, yet after the pleasantries of sharing greetings, we were all rather quiet for most of the four-hour trip.

The journey to my village was on a paved road for the first fifty-five miles. The last forty-five miles were over a dusty washboard dirt road, pocked with numerous potholes. It was uncomfortable and tiring. I sat in the middle, and I was aware that I wasn't the only one who was sweating profusely.

As we drove into Nsiyaludzu Village, I was struck by the profound poverty there. Our loud, lumbering lorry disrupted the pigs, goats and chickens, which were scurrying about everywhere, but the scrawny dogs continued to sleep and the skinny cats simply ignored the noisy old relic. The children wore tattered, dirty rags. The village was littered with dried corn husks, corn cobs, other bits of trash and lots of dung. The huts were in disarray and windowless. It was obvious even to this newcomer that most roofs needed to be rethatched and that the mud exterior walls were also in need of repair. It was the dry season, so it was *hot*, without a breeze, and the smells were pungent and pervasive—not one that was either sweet or pleasant.

Suddenly we were surrounded by a *huge* crowd of adults and children. "*Azungu, Azungu!*" [White people, White people!] was shouted incessantly by the children. They watched us attentively—smiling, running and chattering. Three boys were keeping an old bicycle tire rim rolling with the aid of a stick. Another two boys were taking turns pushing around an old tire. One kid was playing with a homemade toy car made of bent wire. Some of the girls were minding babies, with many of the latter being carried on their backs. I was peppered with a myriad of questions, yet I could only grin and respond to their series of greetings.

Our driver haltingly managed to inform us that my counterpart, *Bambo* [Mister] Chitowe, the medical assistant (a physician's assistant in the U.S. under whom I was to work at the local medical dispensary (clinic), had been called away on an emergency to a neighboring village. All that was known was that a family had been struck by lightning.

After Jere, John and I had unloaded my belongings and wished each other well, I waited patiently for three hours on the narrow roadway, which was more like a path that stretched from the main road to the dispensary. There I was with my suitcase, a footlocker filled with books and a cardboard bookshelf, a two-burner paraffin (kerosene) stove, a few pots and pans, a water filter, two kerosene lamps, a mosquito net provided by the Peace Corps, a narrow bed, an old smelly mattress, a small round table and a chair supplied by the Malawian Ministry of Health. I had no idea where I was going to be staying.

Unexpectedly, the crowd around me slowly parted as a Land Rover approached. The driver was my favorite of the "senior" PCVs who helped complete our in-country training program. Art Weinstein was a veritable prince. He was fluent in Chichewa after his extended term for a third year, and he was knowledgeable and comfortable with many subtle Malawian cultural nuances. I admired him immensely.

I tried hard not to show how glad I was to see him. "*Moni* [Hi], Art. What brings you here?"

"I'm here because of a snafu at headquarters. I've come to deliver the supplies for your clinic." He went on to explain that after our lorry had departed from the PC office in Blantyre, one of the staff members had discovered that all of the clinic necessities for the entire public health program had been left behind. Art's vehicle was one of many which had been dispatched to play catch-up. Mine was Art's second stop. He told me that he didn't have any spare time and wanted to know where he needed to drop off my things.

"This is the place," I said pointing to a spot. "If I heard right, that hut under construction over there will be my mine once it has been completed. I'm here waiting for my counterpart. He's been called away to a neighboring village on an emergency."

After I helped him unload the rest of my stuff, he wished me well and scurried away. Years later, he shared with me what he had written in his diary that evening:

"I will never forget the day I dropped off newly arrived PCV Jack Allison in a grass-thatched, mud-walled house in a remote village. Glancing back at this young man, as I drove away down the dirt road, I worried about his welfare."

That day I could definitely identify with his concerns (which were unknown to me), for I was experiencing what our mentors in training had forewarned: You will find yourself in strange surroundings that no amount of preparation will suffice in easing your entry into a foreign culture and its environs.

Most of the villagers, especially the children, had never seen a white person before, and they were quite curious about and a bit frightened of me. The crowd remained close. Even though the people were rather loud, they were undeniably friendly. Many kept referring to me as *Bwana* [Sir].

Chief Nsiyaludzu emerged from the crowd, introduced himself and tried to have a conversation with me. The chief was toothless, so I was having a difficult time understanding him. He was quite diminutive, shoeless and wore a scruffy old fedora hat which was full of holes. I was embarrassed when he chided me for only being able to say *moni ndi zikomo* [hello and thank you]. No one in the quietened crowd reacted whatsoever.

Mr. Chitowe finally appeared. After we had shaken hands and passed greetings, he apologized by saying, *"Pepani, Abambo* [I'm so sorry, sir]. I was called to the next village because of an emergency."

"What kind of emergency?" I asked. But before he could answer, I added, "How often are you called upon to leave your clinic for an emergency?"

Again Mr. Chitowe apologized for not being there to greet me upon my arrival. He explained that a family of four had been struck by lightning as they were eating lunch together. The parents had been killed outright and both children had been burned significantly. He had treated the children and had arranged for their ongoing care, including follow-up, before returning to the dispensary. He added that it was extremely rare for him to be called away from the clinic.

"We are in the process of building a new home for you within Nsiyaludzu Village. That will take some time. We've arranged for you to have temporary lodging in an abandoned storefront located a half-mile away along the main road."

Mr. Chitowe then commandeered a group of adults and children to carry all my stuff there. He asked about the day's journey as we walked together. After my *katundu* [baggage] and all other belongings had been placed in my new digs, he invited me to dinner. I graciously accepted.

It was dark by the time Mr. Chitowe picked me up. We walked slowly by flashlight and chatted, getting to know one another. I had observed earlier that he was a handsome man with a charming smile and a distinctive laugh. He was clean-shaven and his hair was neatly cropped. He and I were the same size. He was thirty-two, married with three children, but his family had yet to join him since his transfer four months prior. His wife was due to deliver their fourth child any day. He wasn't sure when she and the rest of his family were going to be able to join him in Nsiyaludzu.

Mr. Chitowe had "hired" a local woman as a temporary housekeeper who prepared our dinner. Much later I discovered that he was somewhat of a Casanova, having a bevy of girlfriends in our village and those surrounding ours.

Admittedly, I was in "culture shock on the hoof" at dinner in his small, darkened home. The only light was provided by a small old petroleum jar, filled with kerosene and fitted with a wick. A squadron of bees had infested the chimney, and they were *everywhere* as we dined and chatted. Since Mr. Chitowe totally ignored them, I did my best to do so, too. I could see the whites of Mr. Chitowe's eyes and his white teeth, yet since the walls were dark, it was difficult to see his face clearly. There were no knives or forks, which is typical in any Malawian village.

The meal consisted of *nsima*, the Malawian staple—a big bowl filled with large piping hot cornmeal patties and a small bowl of reconstituted salted sun-dried fish. And those patties! My right hand was not accustomed to food straight off the stove, so I had considerable difficulty in picking one up and transferring it to my plate. (I am a converted left-hander, yet I had been forewarned about *not* touching *any* food with my left hand. The latter is reserved for certain of bodily functions in the toilet. Culturally, even other objects are to be passed with one's right hand, to show respect.) Having never been a fancier of fish to begin with, the smell and taste of the salty fish were overpowering. My appetite dissipated rapidly. I recall wondering how I was going to survive.

I also had erred that evening by drinking a proffered glass of water. The next day I had profuse diarrhea.

As Mr. Chitowe finished his meal, I asked him what his full name was. He told me that it was Gabriel David Chitowe, but that he preferred using his initials, G.D., when dealing with professional issues. Since he had called me Jack, I asked if I could call him Gabriel. He said no. He preferred to be called Mr. Chitowe or Achitowe. He explained that by adding an "A" before someone's name pluralized it to show respect in their culture. I did not challenge him that he had not done so with my first name.

After dinner, we enjoyed a cigarette and a warm beer together. As we continued to chat, I shared with him that I was uncomfortable being called *Bwana*. "Mr. Chitowe, I don't know if you've ever seen any Tarzan movies, but they were incredibly patronizing toward Africans. If there's any way that I could not be called *Bwana*, I would really appreciate it."

Mr. Chitowe had an immediate solution: He explained that his *mfunda* [clan name] was Phiri, and with appropriate respect, became Aphiri. From that day forward we called each other Aphiri. I felt heartened that he was willing to accept me, a stranger, so openly.

Once Mr. Chitowe had walked me to my new home and we'd said our goodbyes for the night, I lit the larger kerosene lamp so that I could write some aerogram letters. Soon my room was filled with moths which attracted a half-dozen large "fighting spiders" which darted wildly around my table. There was also a bat which flew around the room as bats are wont to do.

After hurriedly brushing my teeth and peeing out back, I grabbed the flashlight and tucked myself in under the mosquito net. Within minutes, I heard a strange noise. I flicked on the flashlight, and saw the bat hanging upside-down on the net—fortunately on the *outside*.

It took me a *l-o-n-g* time to fall asleep that first night.

MUSIC ON A CRESCENDO

"Music, once admitted to the soul, becomes a sort of spirit, and never dies."

Edward Bulwer-Lytton

Music has always been an important part of my life. My mother had a lovely untrained voice, and she would break into song frequently, especially when we were in the car on a road trip. I really liked her voice, but I didn't appreciate her singing when we didn't have a choice.

She had quite a repertoire, although her favorites were *I'll Be Seeing You, (I Love You) For Sentimental Reasons, It's Only a Paper Moon,* and *You'll Never Know.* When she heard me singing in the bathtub, my mother decided that I should be a child star. Since I wasn't interested, her arranging for me to have an audition for a local amateur hour was a disaster when I showed no energy for it. A long time passed before she forgave me for letting her down.

Then my third grade teacher introduced the tonette to our class. It reminded me of a very short, plain, black, plastic clarinet. She tooted away with a series of simple tunes—*Row, Row, Row Your Boat, Mary Had a Little Lamb,* and *Old MacDonald Had a Farm*—and promised to give each of us a *free* tonette the next day, including a *free* songbook. I was so excited, for I knew my parents wouldn't have been able to afford either had they been required to pay for them.

When I played the tonette at home, my mother would often get irritated with me. "Stop playing that nasty thing and get in here and

9

help me with your brother!" Robin was ten years younger than I. Because I spent so much time caring for him while my parents worked, I was the only one who could get him to eat and go to sleep for naps and, especially, at night. He also preferred me to feed him his bottle.

I still practiced the tonette whenever I could, and, as a result, I did well in music class. When we moved a few months later, tonette was not offered at the new school. I was really upset, and the lack of support from my parents was palpable. For most of the fourth grade, I had no music instruction.

Upon our next move, I was introduced to the cornet, a foreshortened version of the trumpet. I begged my dad to rent the cornet for me. Reluctantly, he acquiesced. The only proviso was that I was forbidden to practice in our 31-foot trailer.

I took the cornet seriously. I practiced playing it every day and improved steadily. The bandmaster, who taught all three bands—elementary, junior high and high school—took considerable credit showcasing my burgeoning talent.

Those brief days of glory ended when we moved yet again. I was embarrassed when my dad had fallen behind on the rental payments for the horn, and I was reminded weekly at school that if payments weren't forthcoming, I would have to return the cornet. Similarly, my dad received dun notices in the mail three months in a row.

I decided to resolve the issue on my own. A few days before our move, I turned in the cornet. When my dad discovered what I had done, he was livid. "Goddammit, Jack, why in hell did you do that, you ungrateful little bastard? I was going to sell that horn!"

That wasn't the first time my dad had disappointed me. He often made promises that he didn't keep, such as leaving me in the car with my three younger brothers after telling us that he was going to take us the movies. What he did was leave us for hours on end, drinking and playing poker with money that our family simply didn't have. It got to where I no longer had *any* respect for him, and neither did my mother. After a few "rehearsals," she finally threw him out the following month. The ongoing problem wasn't resolved, though, for she let him back in a few days later. It took her another year to finally file for divorce.

THAT MOVE WAS AT THE END of the fifth grade for me, and the fifth move we had made that year. My dad punished me during the sixth grade by not allowing me to rent another cornet. However, things changed at the beginning of the seventh grade. In response to a brief survey requested of all students by the high school band director, Mr. Gene Gorman, I was asked to report to his office after school.

"I see that you've had two years of experience with the cornet," he said.

"No, sir, that's not quite right," I said. "I played the tonette for one year, the cornet for one year, and then took off a year."

"Well, I have a proposition for you. Would you be willing to switch to the baritone? I ask because I don't have a baritone player for the high school band."

"My parents can't afford to buy a baritone!"

"Jack, you would be *renting*, not buying. It's the same with tuba players." I looked down at the floor, not knowing how to respond.

Mr. Gorman tried again. "Are you not interested? The fingerings are the same, and you can still play most of the music in treble clef. And bass clef is easy to learn."

I apologized and reluctantly told Mr. Gorman that my parents wouldn't be able to make the rental payments. He smiled and placed his hand on my shoulder. "Jack, if you're willing to play baritone, the financial issues will be taken care of ... that is, *if* you'll keep those arrangements between the two of us."

I stood up immediately and shook his hand, smiling broadly. This had been my introduction to the proverbial win-win transaction, yet it was so much more. His generosity meant so much to me. I appreciated his having faith in my potential and nurturing my musical talent by giving me free private lessons. Mr. Gorman was the first of many adults who helped me immeasurably along my pathway.

From then on, I was referred to as "the little man with the big horn" on campus. And since I was only eleven and the only baritone player among much older student players, I practiced diligently every day. There was one adjustment that I had to undergo: Although I was a converted lefty, I still played the cornet with the fingers on my left hand. Since this was impossible to do with the baritone, I had to learn to play with my right hand after all.

IN THE NINTH GRADE I REALLY enjoyed singing counter tenor in the high school chorus—that is until my voice changed overnight, which put me back in the band permanently. Mr. Gorman had allowed me to sing with the chorus as long as he could count on me to meet his needs with the band.

Miss Hall was the choral director. She was blond, knock-down gorgeous, and I had a crush on her, as did many of the other thirteen-year-old boys. She also took a lot of extra time with me because I sang the counter tenor parts better than anyone else, boys or girls. We had been rehearsing to participate in the Florida state-wide high school choral contest, and I had two major solos. Then disaster struck. Early in the morning that we were scheduled to board a bus to travel to Daytona Beach for the contest, I telephoned Miss Hall in a panic. I listened as the phone rang and heard the click. "Hello, this is Miss Hall."

I swallowed hard. "[Croak]. Miss Hall? [Croak].

"Who *is* this?" she asked.

"[Croak]. It's Jack, Miss Hall."

"Oh, gracious me! Your voice has changed!"

Her diagnosis was spot-on. I'd gone from a high tenor to a *basso profundo* overnight, and because my voice kept cracking, I literally couldn't sing a note. The young girl who got called upon at the last moment couldn't sing my parts quite as well, so unfortunately our chorus didn't fare as well as anticipated in the state competition.

I didn't sing again in a chorus until my freshman year in college.

THE UNMITIGATED HIGHLIGHT OF MY SENIOR year in high school was marching in the Mardi Gras parade in New Orleans. Parents of band members helped us raise money for the trip by joining in the selling of candies, washing cars and soliciting donations.

The train ride from Avon Park, Florida, to New Orleans was special, for I got to spend a high schooler's dream—some protracted time with our drum majorette. Those few hours of innocent pleasure with her landed me in deep trouble with her football player boyfriend upon our return, yet the gambit was decidedly worth it.

The day before the parade included a bus tour of the city and an introduction to Cajun cuisine and espresso coffee. At seventeen, unfortunately, I was too young and inexperienced to fully enjoy and appreciate what was being proffered. However, the sights of the city were amazing, including the fact that, because of the high water table, the dead are buried above ground. What a festive old city! And the jazz played on the street and in open-area restaurants and bars was spectacular.

The parade was seven miles long and quite challenging, especially because the temperature was in the nineties and our uniforms were made of wool. I was the drillmaster of the band, which meant that I was in charge of getting everyone ready to perform. Since Mr. Gorman had retired, I had a particularly good relationship with the band director, Mr. Vic McMurray. He trusted me to carry out his orders, which we usually decided upon together. At the four-and-a-half-mile mark one of the seventh-grade clarinet players became overheated. As the band marched and played on, I immediately took her out of line to the sidewalk and asked one of our female chaperones who was following along with us to loosen her coat, remove her plumed hat, take her to a ladies room, and splash water on her head, face and neck.

As drillmaster I had been briefed on the parade route and knew that we would soon be turning around for a two-mile march to the end of the parade. Fortunately, the young girl recovered enough to finish the march with the rest of the band.

That evening four of us guys wondered off on our own, dressed in our street clothes. We walked around the back streets not far from Bourbon Street and ended up quaffing a few slow Jax beers in a seedy bar. After walking around some more, we asked a derelict to buy us a pint of cheap whiskey if we purchased one for him.

Unfortunately, the next night on the train ride home when the four of us met in the men's room to share our prized possession, one of the chaperones sensed that something was up, so he stayed in there with us *forever*. Our plan was quashed.

What an incredible experience, though, to have marched in such a special event. It seemed as if the entire populace of Avon Park had shown up the next morning to welcome us home, and the write-up in the local newspaper was laudatory. As far as anyone knew, ours was the only band in all of Florida to have represented our state at Mardi Gras, and that myth was never shattered. *Everyone* was mighty proud!

NOT LONG AFTER MY FIRST SEMESTER had begun at Warren Wilson College, the band director, Mr. John Connet, asked me if I would play cornet with the pep band at soccer games. WWC fielded an outstanding team mainly because of the numerous international players who attended that junior college.

The request was in response to a brief survey the director had elicited from all incoming students. Although I had not played cornet since the fifth grade, I agreed to do so because WWC didn't have a baritone. It took extra practice to get my embouchure ready to play again.

As I was putting up my horn one late afternoon at the end of practice, I was "singing" a difficult run from a march we had been rehearsing when Mr. Connet came around the corner and stopped to listen. "If you can sing it, you can play it!" he said.

I smiled weakly. "Thanks. I'll work on it."

Mr. Connet headed toward the door and then stopped. "By the way, you're a tenor. I need tenors in the choir. Since you'll be required to attend church and vespers, why not sing in the choir?"

I shook my head. "Sir, I've been thinking about going out for soccer. Although I've never played the game, it would give me the chance to learn how to play it and to get in shape."

"Well, you obviously can't play in the pep band and play soccer at the same time. I'll tell you what: drop pep band, play soccer, join the choir, and I'll give you voice lessons."

"Sir, I can't *afford* voice lessons."

"I said I'll *give* you voice lessons, Jack."

On the spot, I dropped pep band and joined the choir. I also made the soccer team but only got to play—and then only briefly—when the Fighting Owls had run up the score.

I ended up taking formal voice lessons for two-and-a-half years, counting an extra six months at UNC-Chapel Hill. Little did I know then just how pivotal those lessons would be for my singing career thereafter—in the Men's Glee Club; with The One-Eyed Jacks rock band; and especially in Malawi, Central Africa, with the Peace Corps.

The UNC Men's Glee Club appeared on *The Ed Sullivan Show* on June 12, 1966.
Ed cut one of the numbers planned by the Dave Clark Five (shown above)
so we could sing another song.

(Photo of the Dave Clark Five on *The Ed Sullivan Show*, CBS Television / Public domain)

THE ED SULLIVAN SHOW

"Music gives a soul to the universe, wings to the mind, flight to the imagination and life to everything."

Plato

"How's the weather up there?" I asked.

Wayne Newton replied, "Send up a weather balloon to find out."

He was 6'2" and twenty-four years old. I was twenty-two and 5'6". I honestly thought he was 6'8", for he was an awkward, lumbering young man.

We appeared together on *The Ed Sullivan Show* on June 12, 1966. He sang one song, and I, three. His was a solo. My contributions were with the University of North Carolina Men's Glee Club.

How in the world did we get to be on television's longest-running variety show that ran for twenty-three years?

It all began at a rehearsal in the fall of 1965 as Toad began: "Gentlemen, I have a question for y'all." Toad was this Southern baritone's disparaging moniker. "Next year will be the 175th anniversary of our Glee Club, and I think that we should do two things in celebration: tour Europe for five weeks and appear on *The Ed Sullivan Show* before we depart."

What followed were a series of epithets and belittling comments from the group at large, until Toad continued, "We've received sizable checks from three former members of the Men's Glee Club—

Jack Palance, Andy Griffith and the CEO of a famous clothing manufacturer—and a pending decision from the producer of *Ed Sullivan*. Would you like to learn more?" Toad was in his characteristic haughty element.

We were *stunned*....Toad had gone far beyond doing the basic "homework" for this proposed venture, and we all wanted to hear more. After a bit more discussion, Toad received an encouraging, resounding, all thumbs up!

Toad was a caricature. Members of the Glee Club didn't actually dislike Alvin—his given name—they just didn't particularly like him. If one word were to describe him, it would be "dumpy." Toad always had an opinion about *everything*, especially about how the Glee Club should be managed, although he was not an elected officer of the group. He was usually summarily ignored, save for a few passing derogatory digs about his uninvited suggestions.

But Toad earned a ton of respect from our director, Doc Carter, and every member of the club, for it was Toad who had elicited the preliminary funding for our trip to Europe, and it was he alone who had approached the producer of *The Ed Sullivan Show*. Furthermore, Toad had secured new clothing for all members from various upscale clothiers in North Carolina: navy-blue blazers, gray slacks, "Carolina Blue" oxford shirts, silk ties, and black leather loafers. What a *coup* by one super-dedicated individual!

I was slated to graduate in June. This new plan had a profound impact on me financially. I had to get another job to raise enough money to be able to make the trip, so I joined a rock band, The One-Eyed Jacks, on my 22nd birthday, December 1, 1965. My savings account ballooned immediately.

Two days after graduation, thirty-nine members of the UNC Men's Glee Club boarded an Eastern Airlines 7:00 a.m. flight from Raleigh-Durham airport to JFK airport in New York City. Others traveling with us were the director and his wife, their daughter and her best girlfriend, an assistant director (just for this trip), a reporter/photographer from *The Daily Tar Heel*, the university's newspaper, and the chaperoning parents of one of our members.

That afternoon we had a tiring four-and-one-half-hour rehearsal at the CBS studio—we were already exhausted from having arisen at 4:30 a.m. The next morning we sang seven songs at St. George's Episcopal Church in Greenwich Village. The women of the church provided an elegant reception for us afterward. We then grabbed lunch in the CBS studio's cafeteria before another three-hour rehearsal, followed by a dress rehearsal for yet another hour. We finally recorded the three songs that we lip-synched during the show, which began at 8:00 p.m.

Ed Sullivan was effusive with his praise of our rehearsal performance that afternoon—so much so that he bumped the second production number by the Dave Clark Five and asked Doc Carter if we could add a third song—something "Southern." This was quite surprising for he had earlier told Doc privately that he wasn't particularly fond of men's choruses.

The first two songs we sang were *Viva Tutti*, an Italian drinking ditty dedicated to young lasses, and *Hey Look Me Over*, from Broadway's *Wildcat*. What was added would be a definite no-no today—a slow, melodic, beautifully arranged version of *Dixie*. Ed Sullivan was ecstatic, as was the studio audience.

After the show we were all frustrated when all the performers on the show gathered on stage to congratulate one another and to share goodbyes. The Glee Club's involvement was ever so brief because we had to leave quickly in order to board our chartered KLM flight to Amsterdam.

When we returned from our European tour, I was amazed to have received a dozen notes from family and friends who had seen our performance, which had included a close-up of my mug.

Earlier in the day I'd had a brief interchange with Ed. "Mr. Sullivan, I thought that you'd be much taller."

He smiled broadly. "I get that a lot."

"I do, too!" I said.

Ed laughed heartily.

Ed Sullivan, c.1955
(Photo by Maurice Carnes LaClaire / Public domain)

THE ONE-EYED JACKS

"If I were not a physicist, I would probably be a musician. I often think in
music. I live my daydreams in music. I see my life in terms of music."

Albert Einstein

Singing with "The One-Eyed Jacks" was a trip—*sans* drugs, that is.
My college career was before marijuana, cocaine, crack, meth and
whatever other drugs came into vogue. The band members' drugs were
the standards of the day—alcohol and nicotine. Our gigs featured plenty
of both—four-to-five hours of sippin' and puffin' along with our playin'.

The five of us had decided on the moniker of The One-Eyed Jacks
because we had been enamored with the title of a slightly-dated film
starring Marlon Brando.

I was lead singer of the band, which included lead guitar, rhythm
guitar, bass, drums, and keyboard. In addition to being lead singer, I
also excelled in my role as first chair tambourine. The downside was
suffering from black-and-blue thighs after each performance, which
were mighty painful by each Monday morning.

We sang the latest from The Rolling Stones, The Beatles, Smokey
Robinson and The Miracles, and with other popular artists and groups
of the day. A definite crowd pleaser was *Unchained Melody* by The
Righteous Brothers, a song that was also a decided favorite when I
eventually sang it many times as a Peace Corps Volunteer in Malawi.

Our first gig was memorable. We played at a fraternity party on the
UNC campus and we were nervous with anticipation. We shouldn't

have fretted, however, for our band was so well received that the participants were mildly upset whenever we needed to take a break.

For four straight hours, I wore an eye patch, which went along with the motif. After we had played an encore to end the evening, I couldn't open my eye when I removed the patch. It was "mattered" shut, as we say in the South. The drummer said that he had an obvious solution (no pun intended): He squirted lighter fluid in my eye to loosen the gunk. Within minutes I was a patient in the emergency department with a frightful case of chemical conjunctivitis (a markedly swollen, tearing, agonizingly *painful* RED eye).

Being rock stars in college was not something members of the band had dreamed of or even thought about, but we became *very* popular with those who heard us perform. What I especially appreciated was that those six months with The One-Eyed Jacks afforded me dates with co-eds I would never have enjoyed otherwise. One night after one of our performances, I took a date to the Arboretum, a magnificent forested "garden" on the edge of campus. Comfortably ensconced on a blanket, sipping rum and Coke (with lime, mind you), she asked me to sing *Chances Are*, a romantic song by Johnny Mathis, a popular singer then and beyond. As I ended the song, a large number of folks surrounding us clapped warmly in the dark, and even asked for an encore. I happily obliged with *Fly Me to the Moon*, which brought on another enthusiastic round of applause.

Yes, social life associated with The One-Eyed Jacks definitely was rewarding.

BECAUSE I'D HAD TWO-AND-ONE-HALF YEARS OF classical voice training in college, I had been reluctant to sing rock and roll. Although I thoroughly enjoyed listening to rock music and even singing it in the shower, I was admittedly a bit arrogant about singing rock in a band. Additionally, I did not want to ruin my vocal cords. Eventually I acquiesced to the lure of money: I made more money in six months singing with The One-Eyed Jacks than I did singing in church as tenor soloist and sectional leader for three full years. I quickly learned how to protect my voice since I needed to be able to sing in church on Sunday mornings, too.

And after a few episodes of drinking too much and staying up far too late, I also learned that singing in church as my "regular" job was much easier with less booze and more sleep the night before.

TWO YEARS PRIOR TO MY JOINING "The One-Eyed Jacks," I had agreed to sing lead in a spoof of The Beatles. Our short-lived band, "DDT & The Roaches," performed two songs in a talent show fundraiser sponsored by the freshman class—*I Want to Hold Your Hand* and *Give Me Money*. I wore an Edwardian wig, sunglasses and an outlandish oversized red corduroy blazer with black splotches. Quite unexpected by us, we brought down the packed house in Memorial Hall and were declared winners of the talent show. *And* the next morning my Beatle-esque wigged, sunglass-bespeckled picture was on the front page of *The Daily Tar Heel*, UNC's campus newspaper.

DDT AND THE ROACHES — The group that out beatled the beatles and bugged everybody, the Roaches, aided by fuzzy-headed, sunglassed DDT (Jack Allison) brought down the house at Memorial Hall Friday night during the Freshman Talent Show.

—Photo by Jim Wallace

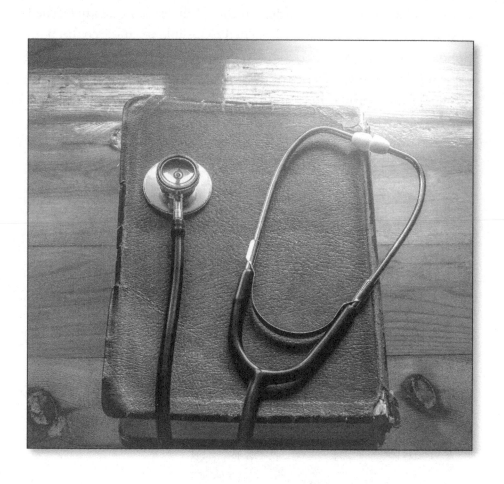

EPIPHANY

"The music is not in the notes, but in the silence between."

Wolfgang Amadeus Mozart

Walking into the office of the Peace Corps recruiter at UNC, on the second floor of the YMCA building which also served as a centrally located convenience store/sandwich shop on campus, was like jamming into a tightly confining box, made smaller by the overwhelming clutter. Ann Queen's desk was in total disarray, with papers, books, pamphlets and brochures stacked, piled and scattered everywhere, without any order whatsoever, and with more of the same on the two folding chairs. If the old adage that a cluttered desk is the sign of a keen mind, Ann Queen must have been a veritable genius. It took her a few moments to hurriedly shuffle and restack enough stuff so that we both could be seated.

Ann Queen always smelled faintly of lavender, and her faded cotton dresses and worn tennis shoes made her look older than 55-ish. On an academic campus she was a most unlikely mentor for me, yet that's what this matronly elder woman immediately became.

"What may I do for you?" she asked.

"I'm interested in learning about the Peace Corps."

"Fine. Do you know where you'd like to serve?"

"Not really, ma'am."

"How about what kind of work you'd like to do?"

"Not yet. I honestly don't know what the options might be."

"Well, we've got to get you squared away. But first tell me about yourself."

I hesitated because I'd never been encouraged to talk about myself. Ms. Queen picked up the slack. "May I ask why you want to join the Peace Corps?" Her warmth was permeating.

"I need a break from my studies," I said. "This is my fifth year as an undergrad, and I'm honestly tired of the grind of studying and working."

"Are you interested in learning a language such as French or Spanish which may be useful to you after your Peace Corps service?"

"Not really. I am interested in having a meaningful international experience, though." I added that because I had met so many international students during my two years at Warren Wilson College before transferring to UNC, I was excited about the prospect of living and working abroad for two years.

She encouraged me to go on.

I felt comfortable in waxing on that I'd come from a poor family. I was a parentified child in that as the eldest of six boys, from age ten onward, I took care of my younger brothers, including changing and washing diapers, making formula and feeding them. Our family had moved a great deal, so much so that I had been in seventeen schools by the time I was in the seventh grade. During my senior year of high school, I made more money with my motorized paper route than my stepfather at his job as an insurance salesman. (He'd had to borrow *my* car for a few weeks that year when his car was repossessed.)

I also told her that I had bought groceries for our family when my stepfather couldn't afford to do so. I added that growing up being called "trailer trash" was compelling motivation for me to escape from the trailer park ghetto.

Ann took her time responding. Her facial expression shifted from engaged to more pensive. I wasn't sure what I had said that caused the change. I hesitated. She paused a few more moments.

"May I interrupt you? I feel the need for us to chat."

"What did I say?" Her statement caught me by surprise.

This time she hesitated. "Jack, I don't usually interrupt someone, especially when I've asked them to relate part of their story. I must ask you if I may share a few comments with you." She paused again. "I really don't wish to be rude."

I shrugged. "Please do. Must be important." I wanted to trust her, yet I still felt uneasy and caught off-guard.

"Okay, let me share a few observations. You know, kids can be so cruel—*life* can be so cruel. However, that was then. Yes, you mentioned, shall I say, your *humble* past. Yet look at how far you have come! That took a lot of strength and resilience.

"Remember where you are today, and what you are exploring. What I'm getting at is for you to please think about letting go of all that *old* stuff, to concentrate on both *now* and your immediate future."

I let her words seep in. We both remained silent. I felt more comfortable— even strengthened—by her unexpected sincerity. I also knew that I needed some time to sort things out. I asked to be excused after firming up a follow-up visit for the next afternoon. Ann smiled her understanding.

That night was sleepless for me, spending what Gestalt psychologists refer to as mind fucking—over-analyzing my situation to gain control over it, yet still failing to do so. Ann's reflections kept my mind abuzz.

I wept a long time in the darkness. I was steeped in melancholia as I kept mulling over my having been raised in poverty and literally not having been afforded the luxuries that most of my high school and college classmates enjoyed. Yes, I was in my fifth year as an undergrad, and fears about my uncertain future were crowding in on me.

Beyond fear, I was feeling a mixture of bitterness and resentment, experiencing the self-imposed pressure of choosing among the Peace Corps, the clergy (I'd been accepted to seminary), medicine (I was majoring in chemistry) or even the Navy (to take advantage of the GI

Bill to help pay for graduate and/or professional studies) as a way of escaping for a while. I was definitely tired of the combined grind of studying, working, and scraping by week after week.

The next afternoon after chem lab I met again with Ann.

"How are you today?" she asked, adding, "I must say you look tired."

"I didn't sleep well."

"What's the problem? Did my comments upset you?"

"No, not exactly. I kept worrying about the choices I have to make soon in order for my immediate future to, how do I say it, take form."

"Then why don't we deal with some specificity. Let's review what the Peace Corps has to offer you."

We sat comfortably next to one another. As we thumbed through the PC materials, I felt a welcoming stimulation that helped to overcome my dreariness caused by lack of sleep. The expansive Peace Corps brochure was a delectable *potpourri* of enticing possibilities.

I was not drawn initially to the African continent. Because of the images on television over ten years before that reflected the brutal winters in Korea during that conflict, I knew that I did not want to be sent there. The countries in Latin America were fascinating, though.

At the end of the brochure, Ann pointed out the mission of the Peace Corps: "To promote world peace and friendship by fulfilling three goals:

1. To help the people of interested countries in meeting their need for trained men and women.

2. To help promote a better understanding of Americans on the part of peoples served.

3. To help promote a better understanding of other peoples on the part of Americans."

I asked Ann to explain the difference between numbers two and three. I thought I understood the second one better.

She thought for a moment before responding. "Number two is to occur while you're serving in your assigned country abroad. Number three will involve your sharing of your experiences with fellow Americans once you've returned back to the States. That's fondly referred to as 'Bringing the world back home.'"

As I mentioned before, Ann exuded warmth. As we chatted about each country of potential service, her enthusiasm was palpable and contagious. She was engaging, knowledgeable, and a superb, patient, reflective listener. She was what I would call an atypical Southern belle—her soft drawl was smooth, throaty and charming, even bordering on alluring, and her vocabulary reflected an unpretentious refinement I found lacking in many of the young, rich, madras-brained co-eds on campus. Her hands announced work in the garden, for her nails were somewhat dirty and unpolished, and her handshake felt a tad rough and chapped.

I asked Ann if she had served as a Peace Corps Volunteer. Although her circumstances, which she didn't proffer, precluded her serving abroad, we lapsed into a spirited exchange about President John F. Kennedy—his inspiring youth, his picture book family, his uplifting speeches, his refreshing wit, his heartening intelligence.

That afternoon we parted on a good note. We were easing into a purposeful professional relationship.

That evening I slept through the night.

Although I didn't see Ann for another week, I did keep wrestling with the substance of our first encounter and her admonishing words. I had a few more turbulent nights of tossing, turning, worrying, regressing into more mind molestation involving anxiety of the unknown. It finally occurred to me that I was having difficulty getting out of the negative box I'd painted myself into. The ultimate issue was whether to choose medicine, religion or the Peace Corps.

TAKING TWO RELIGION COURSES AT WARREN Wilson College was obligatory—Old Testament the first year and New Testament the second. The church at WWC was affiliated with the liberal Northern Presbyterian Church. The irony was that faculty members were far more liberal than members of the student body, in stark contrast with what I experienced once I had transferred to UNC-Chapel Hill.

Having been reared in a combination of the United Methodist Church and varying degrees of "holy roller" Pentecostalism, I was especially drawn to the intellectualism of the church at WWC. The pastor, who also served as Chair of the Department of Religion, was the Rev. Mr. Frederick G. Ohler. He had been an engineering major as an undergrad at Lehigh University, and he was a graduate of Yale Divinity.

Fred was incredibly gifted. His sermons were thought-provoking, often interjecting the holy into the mundane, and dealt courageously with human sexuality, racism, politics, baseball and the arts—in other words, *life*. And Fred's prayers were masterfully poetic, a compelling combination of e.e. cummings, Hemingway and Kerouac—powerful, softly staccato, and dripping with meaning.

I wanted to be like Fred.

Although other students at WWC cozied up to Fred for guidance about how to get into seminary, I chose not to. I remained conflicted about whether to pursue medicine or the clergy as a career choice.

The conflict raged on at WWC. Many an afternoon I would slip out of inorganic chemistry lab to attend Fred's class, "Christ in Contemporary Culture." I read all of the books on the assignment list, and more.

And the conflict raged on at UNC. When I didn't get into Bernard Boyd's class, one similar to Fred's, I would slip out of organic chem lab to "audit" that endeavor from the back of the large auditorium.

One major disappointment occurred when I went to ask Dr. Boyd about whether I needed to apply to any other seminaries. As I stood up to leave, I inadvertently knocked off some papers from his desk. One of those documents was my note to him, requesting a letter of recommendation to Princeton Theological Seminary. I was devastated with angry disappointment, for I had asked for his support six weeks earlier. Neither of us spoke. I left quietly, wondering if I could trust Dr. Boyd to follow through.

However, the next day I received an acceptance letter from San Francisco Theological Seminary, and the very next day another from Crozier Theological Seminary, where Martin Luther King, Jr. had graduated.

The conflict between religion and medicine only became more intense.

OUR THIRD SESSION TOGETHER WAS QUITE upbeat as Ann continued, "John Kennedy changed my life. I respected the man tremendously, for his visionary words mesmerized me, and that's why I chose to recruit for the Peace Corps," she related with ardor. She talked about President Kennedy with a profound reverence beyond the fact that he had been dead for only two years. "Ask not what your country can do for you; ask what you can do for your country," she recounted enthusiastically from President Kennedy's inaugural speech. I shared that I had been enraptured by that speech, too, when I was a senior in high school.

(It wasn't until after I'd been accepted to Peace Corps training that I learned from most of my fellow trainees just how much influence President Kennedy's words had had upon our wanting to serve with the Peace Corps.)

Every evening as I read and re-read in detail about each country in which the Peace Corps operated, I could picture myself in one after the other. After spending many cumulative hours fantasizing about where I might serve, I sought out Ann Queen once again. Our sessions together always left me in elevated spirits, idealistically very much looking forward to making a modest contribution to changing the world, yet always with a pervasive feeling of unease. Why were Ann's perceptive words so agonizing to me? They called to me, Zen-like—Wake Up. Be Aware. Connect with the Present. *Be Present.* Let Go of the Past. Live, Learn, and Don't Look Back.

The night before we met for the fourth and final time, again I didn't sleep well, yet I gradually felt a certain release from being reared in poverty, including a letting go of self-pity. I didn't have a "Come to Jesus" moment. I had a "Come to Jack" encounter. I told myself that it was time to create a new chapter in my life, and what I needed to accept: It was time to grow up, and to be my own person. That short, that simple, that meaningful.

"Ann, I'm having a tough time deciding where to serve."

"Jack, please don't forget that your request is just that. Peace Corps will make the final decision, after taking your preference into consideration."

"That sounds like a mixed message to me."

"Mixed message about what, exactly? My advice is to go with the flow. You have a lot to offer. I'm convinced that you'll do well wherever you'll be placed. Since you're unsure, just go with the flow. And forget not the Peace Corps mantra: 'Be flexible!' That will definitely serve you well!"

I was anxious about making those two final decisions concerning the Peace Corps—whether to join, and if so, where. However, I did finally let her in on my quandary about choosing between medicine and the clergy (to which she said that she wasn't surprised). I joined the Peace Corps to sort out *that* heady decision.

On the last page of the application I simply wrote: "Please send me wherever I'll be needed most."

"THE TOUGHEST JOB YOU'LL EVER LOVE"

"Music produces a kind of pleasure which human nature cannot do without."

Confucius

I found the chapter title above a compelling television advertisement. "Join the world and see the Peace Corps" was yet another TV ad that resonated with me as I contemplated reporting to training.

When I received my acceptance letter from the Peace Corps, I was overjoyed! It was signed by Sargent Shriver, the first Director of the Peace Corps, and is shown on the following page. Eventually, that letter would have both historical and deeply emotional significance.

Initially, I was assigned to teach math and science at a secondary school in Ghana, West Africa. However, soon thereafter, I called Claude Franklin, the PC desk officer for West Africa.

After identifying myself, I said, "Mr. Franklin, I'm calling to see if my assignment can be delayed for two months because I'm a member of the Men's Glee Club here at the University of North Carolina and we're going to be touring Europe for five weeks during the time I've been scheduled to report to training."

He responded in an upbeat, friendly manner which I had not expected. "Not to worry. We'll get you reassigned, for you'll obviously miss the training time slot for secondary education in Ghana. Hmm, your file says that you're amenable to serving wherever you'll be needed most. Is that still correct?"

PEACE CORPS

Washington, D. C. 20525

December 20, 1965

Mr. Earl J. Allison, Jr.
203 Lewis Hall, U.N.C.
Chapel Hill, North Carolina

Dear Mr. Allison:

It gives me great pleasure to invite you to train for Peace
Corps service. Out of a large number of applicants for the
Peace Corps, only a few are invited to enter training. You
are among this group because we think you have the necessary
background and ability.

Over the next few months we will match your abilities to the
needs of the countries which have asked for Peace Corps Volunteers,
giving full consideration to any preference you have shown. As
soon as specific programs have been decided upon you will
receive further information, including a complete description
of your particular country assignment. Your training should
commence during the summer of 1966.

So that we may place you in the most appropriate assignment,
please complete and return the Response to Training Invitation
and the Area and Assignment Preference forms.

You have my best wishes for successful service in the Peace
Corps.

Sincerely,

Sargent Shriver
Director

Questionnaire No. 129623
Enclosures

I was quite happy with his tenor and tone, especially his willingness to accommodate my need to delay my reporting to training. I just didn't know what else to expect.

"Jack, just this morning we began assigning Peace Corps trainees to a newly constituted generic public health program for all four states in Nigeria—the North, the West, the Midwest, and the East. Each state has its own distinct language. Think you might be interested?"

Was I ever! When I asked him to explain "generic" public health, he said three words: "Basic. *Very* basic."

Since I had an abiding interest in pursuing a career in medicine, an assignment in public health sounded far better than teaching math and science, directly from a syllabus, without deviation. I accepted his gracious offer immediately.

Four months later fifty young people, mostly recent college graduates, reported to our three-month Peace Corps training program. As an unabashed extrovert, I made friends readily, and I liked most of them from the beginning. We all seemed to share the quiet, yet strongly held idealistic optimism of wanting to contribute—in fostering peace, understanding and change. What I relished the most was that no one wore that stuff on their sleeve. However, many aspects of PC training were incongruous. The first was the setting. La Jolla, the wealthiest community in California ... *and* the entire country. This was the backdrop for preparing us for a starkly different milieu in the African bush.

Then, after a few weeks of living in the modern dorm at the University of California at San Diego, the students returned from summer break, and the single men trainees were shifted to the old Camp Matthews, a former WWII marine base that had been phagocytized by UCSD as this new campus was constructed. Camp Matthews consisted of remote, dilapidated Quonset huts full of *small* bunkbeds, complete with musty, stained mattresses left over from the war some twenty-plus years earlier. Things were quite different for the single women and married couples—they were ensconced downtown on the oceanfront in the posh La Jolla Cove Motel.

There was inordinate stress involved in our three-month training program because we trainees were under the pervasive threat of being "deselected" if we didn't measure up. Everyone was required to attend bi-weekly, half-day small group sessions led by psychologists from the Western Behavioral Science Institute (WBSI). Of course wily trainees covertly renamed the BS part. Many of these meetings ended up as excuses to attack fellow trainees who were deemed "non-conformists" or "high risk/low gain." Too many of these sessions, under the aegis of sensitivity training, were incredibly brutal:

"How in hell were you ever invited to training?"

"I don't like your know-it-all attitude!"

"Your sucking up to the staff is disgusting!"

It was exceedingly rare for trainees to openly share positive comments about fellow trainees. I kept a low profile and thereby avoided being attacked. I mostly observed those encounters without comment. Not surprisingly, most of the trainees who were identified as having unacceptable behaviors or other negative personality traits were actually deselected at the end of training.

After the initial excitement of getting together, boredom slowly crept in. Lectures and other presentations became repetitive and many times were patronizing, especially comments about how things were going to be *so different* in the village. Many of us quietly began to mumble our displeasure, especially because we had experienced so few hands-on opportunities. One day in my frustration, after yet another mindless lecture, I blurted out spontaneously, "All I want to do is build a goddam latrine!" Immediately I thought that I was in danger of being sent packing. Much to my surprise, the entire training group clapped loudly, and long. Even more surprisingly, the next morning training staff members piled us on a bus, took us out into the country, and joined us in digging for half a day. That jovial, dusty, menial activity was also simple, understated and meaningful. It was a bonding experience for trainees and staff that actually brought everyone closer together.

One of the true delights of PC training for me was singing in a barber-shop quartet, The La Jolla Four. Two of the guys were in the overlapping training group destined for northern Nigeria to work in agriculture and rural development (Ag-RD), and the other two of us were from our public health group. Our training group's favorite watering hole on the weekends quickly became *Danny's Fa*, owned and operated by an outgoing, welcoming Hawaiian and his engaging blonde mainlander wife. Once The La Jolla Four had learned enough songs, we sang there every weekend where we were treated to an unending flow of beer. We were a hit!

Beyond bonding with each other, the best part of training was learning one of the languages we were going to be speaking in Nigeria: Hausa, Yoruba, Pigeon English and Ibo. I studied the latter, a difficult tonal language spoken in eastern Nigeria. Language training was outstanding, as was being apprised of the cross-cultural aspects of African life.

Another tremendous learning experience was spending two weeks of field training in Baja California, Mexico. Although Mexico now welcomes the Peace Corps, it had not yet been invited to serve there during the '60s. Somehow PC leadership successfully negotiated with the Mexican government for us to train at various health departments throughout Baja. I was assigned with a small group of trainees to work at the Centro de Salud in Mexicali. Our Mexican hosts were gracious in welcoming and assuring us that we would have a worthwhile experience. Uniformly discomforting, however, was that we were sworn to secrecy about our being PC trainees.

One particular highlight of working in Mexicali was a puppet show that a fellow trainee (she definitely knew more Spanish than I) and I produced and performed in Spanish for five-and six-year-old children who were about to receive mandatory immunizations as a prerequisite for attending school. The show's message contained simple information about what the "shots" were for, that the procedure would be brief and that their pain would be comparable to that of a mosquito bite or less. The children were enthralled with the puppets, for they really paid attention, laughing heartily at our silly, honest humor. The public health nurses were delighted. "*Mil gracias! Muchicimas gracias!*" ["A thousand thanks! Thank you so very, very much!"]

They credited our unique approach for making the experience far less traumatic for the children, resulting in fewer tears and more efficiency in terms of time and orderliness.

We trainees were pumped! The two crucial lessons for me from this experience were the importance of learning the local language and how utilizing puppetry could enhance learning.

BONDING: PROXIMITY IS NECESSARY TO SHARE experiences, yet the critical element is going through a crisis together. Following our enthusiastic small group debriefing sessions back in La Jolla, an unexpected announcement was made: "There will be an emergency meeting in the large classroom at 10:00 this morning. Please spread the word. This is important!" Staff were busy making sure that everyone would be present.

The training director began with the hackneyed, "I've got some good news and some bad news. What do you want to hear first?"

"Give us the bad news first" was the spontaneous consensus.

The director was blunt. "You're not going to Nigeria."

There was an empty silence as the import of that statement seeped in. He went on. "You're being reassigned because the civil war in Biafra is draining their already depleted GNP for health care and, more importantly, you volunteers would be in danger because of the escalating conflict."

Collectively we were in shock. After the director had begun to repeat himself following a long-winded attempt to convince us that this was the right course to take, he was asked to share the good news. "Six of you single women are going to be reassigned to Niger to work with Muslim women under the broad banner of public health. The rest of you will also be public health volunteers in Malawi—which by the way, is the poorest country in the world."

I remember bobbing my head briefly until I realized something climactic. I turned to the female trainee sitting next to me and asked, "Where is Malawi?" She didn't know either.

After the meeting dissolved, fellow trainee Steve, who was a recent masters level graduate in African Studies at UC-Berkeley, invited us to gather outside under a shade tree for a tutorial. He was impressive in relating to us, without notes or any other props, the basic history, topography and geopolitical background of Malawi, which was formerly known as Nyasaland. The country had actually been renamed by President Hastings Kamuzu Banda, who had returned to Malawi in 1958 after having been away for 34 years in South Africa, the United States, Scotland, Ghana and England, where he had been educated, practiced medicine privately and gradually became involved in politics. Banda was recognized as the most educated Malawian at that time, but he was reluctant to return home to take on the presidency. He acquiesced after being asked the second time. Malawi was granted independence from Britain on July 6, 1964, and became a republic by declaration two years later to the day.

Banda had apparently demonstrated early on in his presidency definite authoritarian tendencies. A cabinet crisis arose in 1964 when several government ministers tried to limit his powers. Banda retaliated by dismissing four of the ministers. Others resigned in protest. The dissidents fearfully fled Malawi.

Steve went on to share that Malawi was about the size of my adopted home state of Florida, with a population of 4.25 million. The country had earned the appellation of "The Warm Heart of Africa," not because of the climate but rather for the abiding friendliness of its people. He said that Malawi was renowned for its beauty, for having the third largest lake in Africa, and for its varied landscape of plateaus, valleys and savannahs.

Located at the southern tip of the Rift Valley, Malawi was an agrarian society, with maize, rice and cassava as the staple crops. Tobacco was its leading export, at fifty percent; others included tea, coffee and lumber. Tourism was a nascent, promising enterprise.

During Steve's low-key yet inspiring talk, I found myself being drawn more to Malawi than I had been to Nigeria.

ONCE WE WERE SWORN IN AS full-fledged U.S. Peace Corps Volunteers, we were sent home for a ten-day break before meeting back up in San Juan, Puerto Rico, for a long, hot, loud, rickety, bumpy bus ride to an isolated PC training camp in the rainforest above Arecibo. We were immersed in a month of learning an entirely different language and contrastive cultural values and customs for Malawi. Again, these facets of our training were absolutely superb. I worked diligently on learning as much Chichewa as I could, and at the end of that intense month, I scored high on the Foreign Service Institute (FSI) exam.

Finally, the foundation had been set for the next phase of this most personal venture. So many facets of training were behind me in one sense yet were continuing to evolve and expand—language, customs and sensitivity. My normal, gregarious, extraverted persona became more contemplative and somewhat withdrawn. As we departed from Miami for Malawi, my hopeful anticipation for a successful tour as a PCV was high, tempered with being a tad fearful of the unknown. I just could not wait to get to The Warm Heart of Africa!

MOTORCYCLES AND BICYCLES

"Music is well said to be the speech of angels."

Thomas Carlyle

Even for those of us who knew how to ride a bicycle, learning to ride a motorcycle was extremely challenging for many. During our two weeks of in-country training and orientation, we were told that we would be issued motorcycles to use to travel to surrounding villages for follow-up and to perform cooking demonstrations. The volunteers in the TB Project already had been provided motorcycles in order to deliver medications and for follow-up visits with their patients. As a rule, PCV teachers were not issued motorcycles.

All the PCVs assigned to the Under-Fives' Baby Clinics were assembled on an open field in Blantyre to introduce us to our new machines and to allow us to learn and/or practice riding them. Since I'd amassed many years on a bike when I was younger, I learned the nuances of transitioning to a motorcycle more quickly than most of the other PCVs. Mine was a 125 cc Honda street bike.

Why not bush bikes or off-road bikes? Because none were available in Malawi.

Bob was one of my buddies who was from the Bronx in New York City. He was even more unsteady on the 90 cc bike he'd been issued. It was painful to watch Bob try to learn how to ride his bike with skill and confidence. Bob required the most time to master riding his motorcycle. He even had difficulty cranking it. He was so unsteady that one (or two) of our instructors had to walk or run alongside him as he jerked his bike around the field. Bob required another half-day of practice before he was issued his machine.

Fate was not kind to Bob. During the first week at his post, while riding to do a cooking demonstration, he hit a rock in the road, went airborne, and landed on another rock. His elbow was cut which became infected a few days later. He had to be treated by a physician—he couldn't work or ride his bike for a week.

During his first year in Malawi, Bob was riding out to do some follow-up visits from his clinic when he ran into a nine-year-old boy who was riding his bicycle. They collided at a T-junction when the boy veered into Bob's pathway. Luckily, the boy wasn't injured seriously, yet the incident drew a large crowd quickly, including the boy's parents who lived close by. A police officer was summoned, and the accident escalated into a major local event. Bob was charged with having caused the crash. Soon thereafter a trial was held; Bob was found guilty as charged and fined $300. The Peace Corps office in Blantyre failed to come to Bob's defense, which was quite unusual. After paying the fine, Bob had to forego his planned vacation to visit the game preserves in Tanzania.

Bob suffered yet another mishap on his motorcycle. While transporting a new PCV he was training to take over his clinic, they slide down in the mud. Fortunately, the young woman on the back was uninjured. Unfortunately, Bob's leg was burned on the muffler, a scar he bears to this day.

Jill McCoy, who was to be stationed close to me, was shaky on the motorcycle. Peace Corps, in their inimical wisdom, decided to provide her with a small lightweight 90 cc Honda street bike. Unfortunately, that machine was much more difficult to maneuver, especially in deep sand.

The differences between the 125 cc and 90 cc bikes were enormous. Eventually Jill did okay with a longer practice session. After a half-day of instruction and practice, she passed muster, although with a few reservations.

Jill was taller than the average PCV. She continued to have difficulty in mastering the lightweight 90 cc street bike. Two months after we had been at our posts, we received invitations to visit a married couple in our group. They lived fifty miles from Balaka where Jill resided and worked. They sent us separate notes since we didn't live or work together. To reach their village was a monumental feat—we had to travel over small remote dirt roads all the way.

Jill asked that I lead the way. For her not to "eat my dust," I rode a bit ahead of her. It was slow going on the terrible roads. Occasionally I would stop and wait for her so that we could check in with one another. The fourth time I did so, Jill didn't appear within a few minutes. I turned off my bike and took off my helmet. When I didn't hear the sound of her engine, I turned around and scurried back to look for her.

I discovered Jill sitting in the road. Her face was bleeding profusely, and she was weeping softly. Her motorcycle was noticeably damaged with the handlebars askew and the mirrors missing.

"My goodness, Jill, are you okay?" She was obviously quite stunned. As I got closer, I could see that she had another laceration on her left elbow.

"Jack, I don't feel so well. I lost control of the bike in some sand. It went down quickly, and my glasses broke. I'm bleeding! Am I going to be all right? Dammit, my elbow is bleeding, too!"

She seemed to be in mild shock. I was concerned that she might have sustained internal injuries. "Jill, take it easy. You're going to be okay. Let me look you over. Let's both take a deep breath and see what needs to be done for you."

Although woozy, she kept communicating well. Her glasses were smashed. That's what had caused the half-inch laceration through her left eyebrow. The cut on her elbow was about two inches long, jagged and filled with nasty bloody debris.

I took off my shirt and undershirt. I ripped up the latter and applied pressure to both wounds until the bleeding was under control. After putting my shirt back on, I took in the local landmarks, for I knew Jill's motorcycle was no longer roadworthy, and that I would most likely be returning soon, with assistance from the PC office, to retrieve it. I pushed her bike off the road and covered it with brush.

Once Jill was able to get up and walk around without assistance, she rode the rest of the way on the back of my bike to our friends' house. Her wounds were scrubbed up without the comforting aid of a painkiller. Her two scars would have been much more cosmetic had her wounds been sutured, rather than healing without stitches.

After her motorcycle was recovered from the bush, the PC office issued Jill a 125cc replacement.

ALTHOUGH RIDING MY MOTORCYCLE WAS EXHILARATING, the helmet kept my hair from flowing in the breeze. That machine gave me the opportunity to be alone and to think about potential projects for my village area, a combination of escape, solitude and creativity. I wrote most of my songs and jingles while riding my motorcycle. Because I didn't have a cassette player, I would ride around longer in order not to forget what I'd written. Repetition was crucial. I also always composed the lyrics and the tune together at the same time.

After I'd had the motorcycle for about a year, I slowly began to question whether it was an impediment to being closer emotionally to the people with whom I lived and worked. Mine was the only motorcycle in my village and the immediate surrounding area. After giving it considerable thought, I decided to turn in my motorcycle on a two-month trial basis.

The PC office provided me with a new British-made Raleigh three-speed thin-tired bicycle. Instead of using the motorcycle to go on cooking demonstrations, I now walked. I was joined by my houseboy who helped carry what was needed, and my dog, Iwe, always accompanied us. My intuition proved to be correct—my social interaction with my African neighbors, friends and colleagues increased immeasurably.

Initially, Achitowe wasn't happy with my decision, for it prevented our riding down to Balaka every Saturday for an ice-cold soda or two. Furthermore, the fourteen-mile roundtrip to the market in Balaka or to visit with Jill occurred only once a week, at most.

The negative fallout from fellow PCVs with motorcycles was harsh at first, yet short-lived. They were fearful that their own motorcycles might be confiscated. In less than a month, no one cared one way or the other anymore. I kept my bicycle.

Image courtesy of *Roche Medical Image & Commentary,* June 1969

Fakhadi: I took this shot because it was
the only time I ever saw him wearing shorts, yet *sans* T-shirt

Conversing with Chief Nsiyaludzu

VILLAGE LIFE

"We are the music makers, and we are the dreamers of dreams."

Arthur O'Shaunnessy

I really enjoyed and appreciated my job in the clinic and in the surrounding villages. It was demanding *and* satisfying. Successes were few in terms of nutritional outcomes, yet I quickly became a realist. Many kids didn't have many nutritional and immunological reserves, and were vulnerable to being smacked down by various, and often consecutive, infectious diseases such as measles, diarrhea, whooping cough, diarrhea, pneumonia, mumps and diarrhea. Yes, diarrheal diseases kill *many* kids in the developing world. Follow-up home visits with the mothers and their children were meaningful as well as fun. And as my Chichewa improved, so did my "hamming it up" while I was teaching.

I must say that living in an African village took a lot to get used to! No matter how many lectures and presentations we'd had in training, the transition was so different from anything I'd ever anticipated or even dreamed. One very important cultural nuance in Chichewa I learned early on is that in order to show respect, a person's name is pluralized: Jack became *Ajacki* (all Chichewa words end in a vowel), Mr. Chitowe became *Achitowe*, his and my clan name of *Phiri* became *Aphiri* and *Mfumu* [Chief] became *Amfumu*.

Along with describing life in the village, perhaps the best reflection of my life then is in the people with whom I interacted:

Although it was totally dark by 6:30 p.m., the light from the full moon was the brightest without competition from street lamps or any other sources. Typically, as I was writing a letter home, *Lozi* [Rosie], a seven-year-old neighbor, would approach my open back door and ask "*Odi?*" [May I come in?].

My response was, "*Odini*" [Please come in]!

Lozi would enter, smile sweetly, kneel, extend her right hand and pass greetings, including the usual polite litany. Then she would ask, "Aphiri, since it's the full moon, will you please come play with us?"

How could I refuse?

The primary school-aged kids in my village were fun to be around. Although they were initially somewhat afraid of me, they accepted me early on, for I was wont to ask them simple questions in Chichewa and they were eager to help me to learn their language. The young girls especially liked to sing and dance outside my hut during the light of the full moon, and I loved singing and dancing a bit with them plus even playing a local version of jacks. Playtime such as this usually lasted for an hour.

LATE ONE AFTERNOON, JILL MCCOY AND I were playing catch with a softball in front of my hut when a small group of boys and girls asked if we would teach them how to play the game. One of the kids had noticed that I also had a bat in my hut. Jill and I agreed and said that if enough kids wanted to learn, we would meet them in a classroom in the primary school. Fifteen minutes later thirty students were assembled, eager to learn the rules.

Jill and I took turns, explaining everything we could as simply as possible. When we went outside to set up makeshift bases, she and I demonstrated how to throw, pitch and hit. Everything was done in a mixture of Chichewa and English—"Chichenglish," if you will. We allowed the kids to practice throwing and hitting, and Jill and I were amazed at how quickly most of the kids caught on, especially since this was their introduction to a totally new experience. We decided to have a trial game, but that's when everything fell apart.

Whenever someone hit the ball, the person who retrieved it would invariably run after and throw the ball at the runner. Jill and I could not get them to modify that behavior, for everyone delighted in hitting the runner with the ball, laughing robustly each time they did it. After repeated attempts to try to get them to either tag the runner or throw them out at first base, we gave up.

Although the kids still wanted to play, I convinced them that soccer would be a better alternative to softball. Unfortunately, the young boys in Nsiyaludzu Village, especially the teenagers, had earned the reputation of suffering from what I later learned to be *amotivational syndrome*, caused by smoking too much pot. I simply could not get those youngsters to organize a team. The good news is that there was a soccer pitch located nearby in Sabwera Village, and the kids in surrounding villages were eager to play.

I was invited to play goalie in our inaugural match. Just as we were getting ready to play, a policeman peddled in on his bicycle and asked to join in. This young man was tall, muscular and imposing, and he could run exceptionally fast for a man of his size. He was assigned to the opposing team.

The two teams were evenly matched. The opposing goalie and I had saved two goals each in a game that lasted an hour. In the waning moments, the large policeman came thundering toward me on a breakaway. As he approached with impressive, agile moves, I braced myself for a major collision. Instead, he feinted one way, I took the bait, whereupon he tapped the ball lightly into the corner of the goal.

Our team lost 1-0, but everyone was pleased that a new tradition had been established in our immediate area. Those matches became regularly scheduled events which drew large crowds, with other teams joining the fray.

"*Fakha! Fakha!*" That was the sound of a mother calling for her little two-and-a-half-year-old boy who would show up in my hut any day that my back door was open. This never failed to make me smile. His name was unusual—*Fakhadi*—and his nickname was *Fakha*. I was convinced that neither his mother nor anyone else made any connection with how his name might be (mis)interpreted by outsiders. He always wore a ragged T-shirt and never anything else, and he perpetually had a runny nose. Fakha never said one word to me even though I always chatted jovially with him. He had a deceptively large potbelly; along with thinning red-tinged hair, both signs indicative of kwashiorkor, a form of protein-calorie malnutrition. These facets improved after I'd convinced his mother to add peanut flour [*ufa wa mtedza*] to his maize porridge. Fakha simply loved to grin and stare at me each time he appeared, for he was fascinated with me, and he was indefatigable. Whenever his mother realized that he had wandered off, she would shout his name loudly and repeatedly, although I'm sure she really knew where he was. I actually looked forward to his brief visits, and I was most appreciative that he went outside when he needed to pee. He always left little puddles in my backyard.

Achitowe was not only my Malawian counterpart, he was also my boss. He and I bonded from the start, and we spent a lot of time together after work. His wife didn't appreciate his slipping around at night to visit with a host of women in the area. Malawians refer to this in English as being "movious." Achitowe was most patiently helpful with my determination to learn Chichewa. He was such a superb teacher that I was successful in nominating him to be a part of a group of Malawian language instructors who went to Tucson, Arizona, to teach the group of public health volunteers that ended up replacing our group. Achitowe wasn't quite sure how old he was, for even today there are no birth certificates issued in Malawian villages. He explained to me that the British employed a standard protocol for when a child was allowed to begin school: Whenever he or she could bend their arm over the crown of their head and touch their other ear.

During weekdays I would awaken at 6:00 a.m. My houseboy would serve me a cup of tea before I shaved and bathed. I had helped erect a bathing area next to my hut which consisted of grass-reed walls and a soak-pit in one corner. Each morning I paid two girls to fetch me two pails of water. One was heated for my ablutions; the other was boiled for my drinking water, for my chickens, goats and pigeons, and for washing dishes. When I looked in the mirror while shaving I was amazed at how pale I looked since all the faces I saw each day were black.

THE LOCAL BREWMEISTER WAS NAMED *ADEKESA*, and he brewed *the best* village beer in the surrounding area. He wore a mustache, unusual for Malawian men. He always wore dirty shorts, a ragged T-shirt and a filthy cap, and he chain-smoked TomTom cigarettes, which were the vilest, strongest and worst smelling cigarettes in the country. He was wont to bum cigarettes from me until I started bumming TomToms from him. He then started referring to me as "the cleverest one" in his broken English, for he always insisted on speaking English with me, even as I improved with Chichewa on a steady crescendo. Adekesa was a dear friend who never charged me for beer.

OUR VILLAGE DRUNK WAS AN OLDER woman who lived just behind my chicken coup. I never knew her name—I simply always called her *Amai wanga* [*Mai wanga*, pluralized for respect, means My Mother]. Although poor and unkempt, she was actually quite attractive for her age, considering how much she abused her body with alcohol without eating properly. Occasionally I would walk over to chat with her as she prepared her paltry dinner, and I would invariably see her at Adekesa's beer joint where I always bought her a small gourd of village beer. We liked and respected one another, and we had fun socially. I never asked how she supported herself.

PETER BROWN WAS A COCKNEY LONDONER who had spent some years in Southern Rhodesia (which eventually became Zimbabwe), where he was a laborer. One drunken night while still working in Rhodesia he fell into a deep pit, fracturing a hip. Since he never had reparative surgery, Peter walked with a pronounced limp. He also exhibited a perpetual two-to-five days of scraggly beard, and he always had deeply blood-shot blazoning blue eyes as well as copious brown dust under his nostrils from dipping snuff. He wore an open short-sleeved shirt with snuff sprinkled all over his chest, filthy shorts, sandals in disrepair and a dusty old black beret. Peter owned an aged white Peugeot sedan and hired out his car for trips near and far, for which he always demanded,

"*Poyamba, ndipatseni ndalama!*" ["Please pay me first!"] Peter was fluent in Chichewa. He had paid a high bride price up north for his young wife, *Dorote* [Dorothy], who was beautiful, articulate and a no-nonsense woman. They had a darling toddler. Peter was another dear friend who shared many a beer with me, for he certainly liked to drink!

Although I am short (5'6" back then; 5'2" today), I was relatively tall compared to most Malawians. I "towered" over *Amfumu Nsiyaludzu*. He didn't own any shoes. Periodically he would walk throughout our village, shouting out important announcements, such as when the next funeral would be held (if someone had died during the night) and when the next village court case was scheduled. Amfumu only begged food from me once. He had popped by my kitchen as I was slicing into a piece of fresh beef liver. We both noted that here were many live liver flukes in the organ. When I mentioned that I was going to throw away the liver, the chief insisted that I give it to him and his wife because their cupboard was bare. I gladly agreed, after providing the obligatory safeguards to prevent their being infested.

One Sunday morning I noticed that a half dozen men were conversing casually in the chief's front yard (which was my backyard). I was invited to join them. Amfumu asked me how far my home was from Nsiyaludzu Village. When I explained that I had flown over the ocean in an airplane to get to Malawi, he said, "*Uuukooo!*" in a very long, high-pitched voice. In Chichewa *uko* means *there*; however, the farther away something is, the longer and higher the word is pronounced, and most of the time with an arm slowly arched up and down as the word is said.

A Lancastrian from Manchester, England, John Winfield was an Associate Principal Health Assistant stationed in Blantyre. He became my best British friend and one of my best overall. We met when I was visiting Blantyre on other business. I had dropped by to meet John to discuss some projects I'd had in mind for my village area. We hit it off immediately. John was amazingly cooperative in helping me procure two latrines each for our dispensary, primary school and market, and borrowing a brick-making machine from a famous priest/inventor so that we could complete three other local projects—to build a small shelter next to the dispensary so that mothers could secure reprieve from the weather, to build a house for the local health assistant, and to protect a spring water supply.

John and I spent a great deal of time together after working hours, drinking beer and sharing stories. His wife, Kate, was not happy with this arrangement, for they had two young boys at home, and I was single.

The local "witch doctor" was a legend long before I arrived in Nsiyaludzu Village. In fact, when Art Weinstein, a seasoned PCV, was searching for possible clinical sites for our newly conceived under-fives clinic project, he was directed to *Dokotala Tomasoni Paizoni's* compound, located east of the main road and far into the bush, rather than west and a short distance to the dispensary where Achitowe and I worked. The translation of the good doctor's name is Thomas Poison. That was obviously not a deterrent to the myriad of patients he treated with his pharmacopeia of traditional medicines. When I received a note from this *sing'anga* [traditional healer], inviting me and Achitowe to come for tea on a Sunday afternoon, after confirming with Achitowe, I accepted enthusiastically. We were also joined by Jill, the PCV from Balaka.

Apaizoni's compound was quite impressive. It was large, isolated, immaculately clean, and operated by his eight wives, aged forty-five to sixteen, who were in red uniforms donned with blue trim, white collars and nurses' hats. The eldest was definitely in charge, for they lined up quickly when she barked orders. The fourth eldest later quietly volunteered that Apaizoni only now slept with the youngest three, favoring the youngest.

Tea with scones was delightful, and the three of us also appreciated the extensive tour which included the pharmacy, complete with an explanation and derivation of each powder and liquid. We were weary by the time we departed. Dr. Paizoni made a proposition beforehand: He vowed to have all of his under-five aged children—and there were a large number of them—seen by me in my clinic *if* Achitowe and I promised to refer cases to him, especially those involving hexes and other forms of witchcraft. We shook hands to seal the deal, and all three parties followed through willingly.

Nsiyaludzu Village reminded me a lot of southcentral Florida, where I graduated high school. The weather was subtropical, with bananas and plantains instead of citrus groves. Because no huts had a source for heat, winters were quite chilly, exacerbated by what was called *chiperoni*, a drizzly, misty rain that wafted in southeasterly from Mozambique during the cold, dry season. Because we were in the southern hemisphere, June and July were quite uncomfortable. The rainy season began in December and lasted until May, usually on a gaussian curve. Although not a monsoon rainy period, it could still rain sometimes for days on end.

AFTER I HAD BEEN IN MALAWI for about a year, I received an unusual letter in my post office box in Balaka. The three Catholic priests with the Catholic Church in Balaka had invited me to dinner one week hence. Even though a fellow PCV lived and worked nearby in Balaka, she had not been invited to dinner with the four of us males.

Although I'm not a Catholic, I relished the invitation. Catholic clergy had the reputation of being stalwarts in learning Chichewa exceedingly well—for delivering sermons, praying, reading scriptures, leading confession, counseling and visiting with parishioners—*far better* than members of other denominations.

The evening was quite pleasant—good food (Italian has always been my first favorite cuisine), good fellowship (we conversed in Chichewa since Italian and English weren't part of the mix), and good wine. I had brought a bottle of Portuguese Mateus Rosé that I had purchased from an expatriate merchant along the border with Mozambique the weekend prior on my way back from visiting with a PCV located near Dedza, some seventy-five miles to the north. The four of us ended up consuming over five bottles of wine.

The wine certainly "improved" my Chichewa because I became less and less inhibited the more we drank. I recall trying to remember the Chichewa word for election, muttering "election" to myself, when one of the priests called out *elezione*! That's how much of the night progressed. We definitely enjoyed each other's company, yet I never saw those gentlemen again in the intervening two years.

The following year word got around that an Italian layman laborer associated with that church began displaying bizarre behavior, including touching the breasts and bottoms of the nuns. A few days later he died of rabies. The inflicting animal was never identified.

MY AFRICAN DOG

"Music is my refuge. I could crawl into the space between the notes
and curl my back to loneliness."

Maya Angelou

How I met a German Shepherd named "Hank" is truly amazing, and what evolved thereafter, even more so. But forget that name, for he was soon given a new one.

As a U.S. Peace Corps Volunteer (PCV) who had only been in the country for four months, I had ridden my motorcycle into Blantyre, the commercial capital of Malawi, to record my second health education song. I was on my way to the Peace Corps office to pick up my cycle after the recording session of *Ufa wa Mtedza* (translated loosely as "The Peanut Butter Song") which, much to my surprise, became the number one song in Malawi for the next three years—yet that's *another* story!

Within a block of reaching the PC office, I noticed a couple walking toward me with a *beautiful* dog on a leash.

"*Nice dog!*" I exclaimed.

The young man looked at me and smiled. "Want him?"

"You're joking, right?" I asked.

"No. He's yours, if you want him."

Quickly they explained that they were PCVs who were leaving Malawi after the first year of their two-year tour as secondary school teachers because their marriage had melted down. They had been living on Likhoma Island within Lake Malawi, and apparently spending too much time alone together had done them in. They had not been afforded the luxury of the poet's admonition: "Let there be spaces in your togetherness...."

When I expressed my ambivalence—yes, I would *love* to accept the dog, yet I had ahead of me a hundred-mile trip back to my village *on a motorcycle*—they both chimed in that he was facile at riding on the cycle and simply showed me what to do.

After putting on my helmet and cranking up, I patted the gas tank and said, "Up, Hank!" He hopped up at once, put his paws across the handlebars, then turned around and licked my face. I was stunned, yet incredibly happy that I suddenly possessed such a fantastic dog.

The trip back to Nsiyaludzu Village was *not* uneventful. It was long and tiring, similar to when I had been driven there by lorry four months earlier for my new assignment. The differences were stark: instead of the stifling cab of a loud, smelly, rusty, uncomfortable Bedford truck, I was riding on a motorcycle in the open fresh air, albeit with a dog in my "lap," fearing what I would do were he to suddenly jump off at forty mph. Being scared kept me hyper-alert, especially for the first half-hour. Yet because Hank was calm and relaxed, I became more at ease as our trip progressed.

Then he whimpered and licked my face, notifying me that he had to pee. When I pulled over, Hank ran across the tarmac to chase a ferret. As I ambled into the luxuriant woods and commenced "to shake hands with the unemployed," as one of my college roommates referred to taking a leak, I suddenly realized that I was not alone. I was surrounded by a troop of baboons! There I was, holding onto my claim to fame, when I noticed something move slightly. When I looked around, I was indeed surrounded, the gray fur of the baboons blending in with the enveloping brush.

I stood very still, yet slowly made eye contact with many members of the troop. There were females with babies either suckling or at least hanging on. What appeared to be the alpha male stared at me, although his eyes were not menacing. He was closer than fifteen feet away, with a few others even closer. After a few long moments he grunted lowly, began to move away, and the others gradually began to follow him, their big red arses disappearing as I finally finished my business.

Hank then burst into the circle and began to bark perfunctorily, although he didn't seem eager to pursue the baboons. When we resumed our journey back to Nsiyaludzu Village, I kept imagining what would have become of me had they felt threatened and decided to attack. Scary stuff, indeed.

I was definitely appreciative of the fact that Hank's previous owners had taught him to ride on the motorcycle as a pup. Interestingly, that trip was the only time he ever rode with me. What a strikingly beautiful dog! At ninety pounds, he weighted almost as much as I. (Since arriving in Malawi, my weight had dropped from 135 to 115 because of a bout with malaria, recurrent diarrhea and marginal nutrition.) His coat was clean and shiny, and it was obvious that his owners had taken excellent care of him.

Since I did not like his given name of Hank, all the way home I nuzzled him and cooed his new name, "Iwe," pronounced "EE-way." That word in Chichewa, a Bantu language akin to Swahili, is the familiar form of "you," reserved mainly for kids *and* lovers—or as a derogatory term toward other adults. Whenever I would call out "Iwe" when it was time to feed him, half the children in the village would show up at my hut. Years later my wife was not initially amused when I called her Iwe as my special term of endearment for her.

Iwe and I bonded outright. He accompanied me everywhere, especially when I made cooking demonstrations in surrounding villages or my own. We were inseparable. He slept on or beside my small cot. And although he was incredibly gentle and loving, Malawians were intimidated by his size and therefore gave him a wide berth.

Iwe [You] loved to ride on my motorcycle!

One memorable day, Iwe almost got both of us killed. It was a Saturday, and I was sweltering in my hut while getting caught up with paperwork from my under-fives baby clinic, when a neighbor informed me that one of my patients was dying at the local clinic. I rushed afoot the eighth-mile to pay my respects. The infant had measles and was severely malnourished. He was covered with calamine lotion, a *ghostly* sight, and he had labored respirations. He died within minutes of my arrival.

As I joined the mothers in grieving and expressing our sympathies to the dead child's mother, we were interrupted by a loud commotion outside.

Two men had been squatting under a shade tree, serenely getting stoned on a dried cornhusk-wrapped marijuana stogie, when Iwe relieved himself. First, he cocked his leg, whizzed a tad on the tree, took two steps and squirted more urine on the first African's back, then finished emptying his bladder on the second man.

I was horrified! Although Malawians tend to be polite to the point of being obsequious, those who are drunk or stoned are not, especially when provoked.

The men began swearing loudly and chasing the dog angrily. At first Iwe appeared to be playful, yet quickly ran home when they began to hurl stones at him along with a myriad of vulgar insults. Fortunately, both gentlemen calmed down when I offered to buy them a village beer.

The only other trouble Iwe got into was when he played too vigorously with a baby goat and the goat subsequently died. The owner was livid, yet he was sober, so we were able to sort things out without shouting, swearing or stone throwing. It's remarkable what twice the value of a dead goat can do to enhance international relations.

Iwe and I were together for over two-and-a-half years. He was fiercely loyal, yet never fierce. Not once did he ever growl at me. He had an uncanny sense of "friend or foe," for he was accurately selective about at whom to bark and those whom he would greet enthusiastically. Would that I were that discerning, then and now.

When I returned home after my three-year tour with the Peace Corps, I gifted Iwe to the PCV who replaced me in Nsiyaludzu Village, and when she left after her two years there, she passed him on to Mr. Chitowe. Iwe was a most reliable sentry and a loving, lovable friend who died peacefully in his sleep during his thirteenth year.

Discussing prolonged breastfeeding practices with Achitowe and Amfutso, a local businessman

CROSS-CULTURAL ISSUES

"Love is friendship set to music."

Jackson Pollock

THE INVITATION:

Toward the end of my clinic one afternoon, Mr. Chitowe made an unexpected appearance. "Chief Kauna has invited us to have some beers on his veranda after work this evening," he told me.

"Thank you very much, Aphiri. That'll be fun!" I mused that this would be a first-time event for me.

Chief Kauna was an affable man who was always polite and pleasant with me. His village was close by, directly across the main road from mine. The chief was diminutive—that is, shorter and thinner than I—and he was outgoing in a low-key manner. He also had a unique characteristic—he never once ever made eye contact with *anyone*.

Within an hour we had arrived at Chief Kauna's hut, which was quite small (that means smaller than mine), windowless and in need of a new thatched roof and other obvious repairs. His veranda was short and quite narrow. He had been joined by two other chiefs, Kamanga and Sauwa, from nearby villages. I was mildly surprised that my own headman, Chief Nsiyaludzu, wasn't among the invitees. The three chiefs were seated on chairs side-by-side, and they were well on their way to becoming drunk.

When Achitowe and I came into view, we heard Chief Kauna shout to some boys to fetch two more chairs. The five adults passed greetings and related pleasantries until the chairs arrived. Mr. Chitowe and I sat in the small yard, facing the three village headmen.

I took my time with the gourd of village beer I'd been given. *Mowa* is chunky, and the bits and pieces took lots of getting used to. I could never develop a taste for it. I only drank it to fit in socially with the villagers—plus there was the fact that it *always* gave me diarrhea. Mr. Chitowe, on the other hand, was more than eager to imbibe his beer, which resulted in his becoming tipsy rather rapidly.

What really caught my attention was intermittent tittering from within the chief's hut, which eventually became quiet giggling, followed by muffled laughter. Because the three chiefs and Mr. Chitowe were talking so fast, plus the fact that their tongues were thicker from the beer, I wasn't sure what was going on until everything got quiet as Chief Kauna began to speak:

"Again, we welcome you, Ajacki."

"Thank you very much, *Amfumu* [Chief]," I responded.

The giggling increased, and it sounded most definitely feminine to me.

The chief continued, "We Angoni have an ancient tradition of welcoming strangers, Ajacki. We also try to take care of the basic needs of these strangers."

I didn't quite understand the last part, so I had to ask Mr. Chitowe to translate for me. The chief paused as Mr. C. filled me in.

Whereupon Chief Kauna snapped, *"Atsikana!* [Girls!] Come out here now!"

Three lovely young ladies appeared slowly from the unlit room behind the cracked door. They were fifteen or sixteen—it was hard for me to tell—yet they appeared girlishly innocent. They continued to giggle among themselves.

The chief then went on a *long* monolog, repeating himself at least two more times, before he invited me to choose from among the three to have a companion—"A need that every man must have fulfilled."

Although I didn't get every word he was saying, I most assuredly got the gist.

I panicked! We trainees, during our protracted training period, and we volunteers, once we'd been sworn in, were reminded, too, too often that we were *not* to engage sexually with any Malawians, period.

My exit that evening, *sans* new paramour, was awkwardly embarrassing. My guests were showing me profound respect. I felt caught in a bind. Although I was unwilling to accept their graciousness, out of fear of being discovered by the Peace Corps office and subsequently being sent home, this was something I just did not want to do, but neither did I want to offend them. I blathered on in halting, broken Chichewa that I very much appreciated their gracious, thoughtful offer, but fibbed that I had a wife in Niger, and that she would not be happy to discover the proposed arrangement during her upcoming visit.

The three chiefs reluctantly accepted my "excuse," yet little did I know then that I would soon be visited by a PCV from Niger, a woman I had dated a few times during training. Upon her arrival she was greeted by all the surrounding villagers as "Ajacki's wife from Nigeria!"

At least the two countries are contiguous.

THE CONFRONTATION:

Within a few months after my arrival in Nsiyaludzu Village, three young men about my age visited with me after dinner for three nights in a row. All three were primary school teachers from surrounding villages, and they spoke good English.

Our conversations were cordial, pleasant and protracted and mostly dealt with our backgrounds, which sports teams we were following, and a little about hopes and plans for the future. During the third evening, I sensed that they had something important to discuss because each one would pause a long time before continuing the conversation. Finally, one of the chaps asked, "Is it true that you are encouraging nursing mothers to breastfeed their babies for as long as possible, even up to two years and beyond?"

"Yes!" I answered enthusiastically, and then lapsed into a mini-lecture on the wonders of breast feeding, including protected immunity from the mother during the first six months of the baby's life, plus added hydration, protein and calories. The men waited patiently until I had wound down, then one of them presented their plea:

"Ajacki, would it please be possible for you to limit the time that you suggest to these mothers to no more than one year?"

"Why, gentlemen?" I inquired.

I was then apprised that when Malawian women, once they realize that they've become pregnant, stop having sexual relations with their partner *until the baby is weaned*. They were aware of the term *ntsempho*, literally translated as "late," but with the added "village" meaning of "the disease that a baby will develop if it is weaned too soon." I went on to explain that Western medicine would deem it as protein-energy undernutrition and explained the difference between marasmus and kwashiorkor: maramus occurs in younger children as a result of loss of muscle mass and subcutaneous fat due to severe malnutrition, while kwashiorkor is a form of severe protein malnutrition seen more commonly in older children. I went on to add that these kids get enough calories from carbohydrates, yet don't receive enough protein in their diet. I even added the original definitions, which were similar to the local one: "the sickness the baby gets when the new baby comes" or "the disease of the deposed child."

When I finally concluded with my long-winded explanation, I'd become increasingly aware that the longer I talked, the more their eyes became vacant. They had not come for a lecture.

Compromise was inevitable. The three gents were quite pleased when I promised not to recommend any more than one year of breastfeeding.

PARTY ON!

"Music is the mediator between the spiritual and the sensual life."

Ludwig von Beethoven

Mzuzu was beckoning! The regional headquarters of the Northern Region, Mzuzu is the third largest city in Malawi as well as the cultural center of the Thumbuka tribe. The local language, Chithumbuka, is the second indigenous tongue to Chichewa.

Why was I going there with so much anticipation?

When I received a postcard inviting me to a party in Mzuzu, I was totally surprised, yet quite eager to attend. Since the USA's Independence Day and that of Malawi are only two days apart, some enterprising Peace Corps Volunteers up north had declared that what was warranted was a bipartite celebration. Three PCV secondary school teachers in Mzuzu had divvied up the mammoth task of inviting every PCV in the country, which included enlisting fellow helper volunteers from both the TB project and our baby clinic project. One line on the postcard stated that donations would be graciously accepted at the party to cover expenses.

After living alone in Malawi for six months, I was ready to party down! On July 3rd I rode my motorcycle all day to Ntchisi to meet up with my best PCV buddy, Bill Schmidt. Those hundred and seventy-five miles, over mostly very rough dirt roads, took me ten hours to traverse. An added treat was to get to check out Bill's clinic facility and his house in the village. Both were much better appointed than mine.

Bill and I personified the concept that opposites attract. He was a staunch conservative Catholic; I was a loosely liberal Presbyterian. Bill was a virgin, saving himself for marriage; I was neither. The things we shared, though, were a strong work ethic, our fondness of the Malawian people and their culture, and our individual creative approaches to saving babies' lives and improving the well-being of villagers in the area where we worked. Whenever we got together, we had spirited yet congenial conversations which were usually enhanced over several slow brews.

The next morning we set out a bit late for Mzuzu, having been delayed by an unexpected, cordial visit by Bill's chief. Actually, he had come to borrow money from Bill. These interchanges are difficult to rush in Malawi, for they involve a series of prolonged greetings and other polite chitchat before the substance of the meeting can be broached.

The twelve-hour, hundred and eighty-five-mile trip to the Northern Region was even rougher than the day before because of so many more steep hills to negotiate. Bill and I arrived after dark—cold, exhausted, hungry and mighty thirsty. Once we got through the crowd, we both immediately chugged a warm beer and got a good start on our second one.

The party was wild and crazy! There were at least a hundred volunteers in attendance—I was told that perhaps that many had already departed—and most had been imbibing since early in the day. The music was loud, causing everyone to shout in order to be heard. Many were dancing outside, although it was difficult to discern with whom. Both sides of the duplex were overflowing with PCVs who were going in and out constantly. The outside area around the building was also quite crowded. As I squeezed into one side of the duplex to check out the women, then did the same on the other side, I noted that Bill was the only person I actually knew there. I was unable to locate him again that night.

The primary libation was bottled beer from neighboring Zimbabwe and Zambia. Except for a few packets of potato chips and several large bowls full of unshelled peanuts, there was nothing to eat. It was the first party I'd attended in Malawi that didn't include any Peace Corps staff members. Initially, I was surprised that not one Malawian was there. There were two plausible reasons. The first was that the Malawian counterpart teachers had gone back to their respective villages to celebrate Malawian independence with family and friends. The second was that I got a whiff of the distinct aroma of marijuana. Pot was strictly illegal in Malawi, and the punishment for getting caught partaking of it included being terminated from the Peace Corps immediately, plus the definite probability of doing jail time before being allowed to depart.

Housing for the PCV secondary school teachers was the same for their host country counterparts—a duplex in which both sides featured a small living room-dining room combo and a small bedroom. The kitchen and the latrine were in a small line of similar facilities out the back door. The furniture was identical to mine, except for lamps because they at least had unreliable, intermittent electricity.

While I was standing in line for the latrine, a cute blond behind me named Rhonda brushed by, tapped me on the shoulder and introduced herself. After a very brief chat, I relinquished my turn to her. When I emerged from the latrine, she was still there. She suggested that we go inside together.

Because we had to wait for some people to come out before we could enter the duplex, we exchanged pleasantries. Rhonda was noticeably tipsy, and I was well on my way to joining her. I was eager for some female companionship and she seemed amenable to spending some time with me.

Rhonda shared that she was an only child from Seattle. Her father was a professor of public health and she was disappointed that the Peace Corps had assigned her to be a teacher instead of doing the kind of work our group was performing.

It was incredibly *crowded* inside, with light provided by a myriad of strategically placed candles. The rock music was even louder, with no room for dancing indoors.

Rhonda grabbed my hand and led me to where the beer was stashed. Once we'd opened the bottles, she led me into the bedroom where all the coats had been placed. I was turned on by her subtly aggressive way of getting us alone together.

We flopped down on the coat-covered bed and had just begun to make-out when the door burst open. We were rudely interrupted by her irate husband—I'd just met her some twenty minutes earlier, but I'd had no idea that she was married.

Fortunately for me, her husband directed his considerable ire toward Rhonda, which allowed me to quickly slip by him and out of the bedroom. I did notice that she was *not* wearing a wedding ring. I could also tell by his loud accusatory language that this was not the first time that Rhonda had chosen to seek companionship outside of their marriage. I was obviously worried that this large, muscle-bound man might decide to come after me.

So rather than die at the hands of a crazed, drunken husband, I hopped on my motorcycle for the two-day return trip home. It was winter in Malawi, so the cold air helped to sober me up rapidly.

The journey back to Nsiyaludzu Village was punctuated that night by warthogs that ran in front and alongside my motorcycle—as did a leopard for two measured miles. I dared not stop, even though my bladder was *full*.

Party On!

Mid-morning the next day, I had a flat tire. Fortuitously, it occurred just as I was approaching a small garage in the middle of bloody well nowhere. It still took a long time to get the tube repaired.

Later, as nightfall was descending, I was cold, weary and starving—I had not eaten since breakfast the day before. Also, I was dangerously low on both money and petrol. I decided to spend the night at an African rest house, something never done by white people—Brits, this is—save for PCVs.

Kwa Ujeni was a typical African guest house. The translation brought a chuckle, for it means "The Home of Thingamajig." When I asked the proprietor if indeed his surname was Ujeni, he burst out laughing. The lobby also served as the dining room which contained four small wooden tables; eight rickety wooden chairs; four tattered, slightly soiled tablecloths; a freshly waxed red-stained cement floor; dirty whitewashed walls; and a few randomly scattered tacked up objects thereon, including an outdated calendar and two small faded black-and-white photos. Only one dim light bulb hung down from the splotchy tan ceiling, which was discolored from the dust and dirt.

After negotiating a lesser room rate than proffered, I noted that the place smelled pleasantly of curry. I ordered a modest African meal of curried goat meat with *nsima*, the Malawian staple. I couldn't afford something to drink, and I knew not to drink the water. I was concerned that I was becoming dehydrated.

It felt so good to be out of the cold night and off the motorcycle. My butt was terribly sore from riding so many miles on washboard roads, as was my back over the area of my kidneys bilaterally. I was exhausted.

Just before my order was served, a precious eight-year-old little girl brought a basin half-full of warm water, a small remnant of soap and a small dirty, damp towel so that I could wash and dry my hands. Her timid smile and bright eyes warmed my heart. She was pleasantly surprised when I thanked her in Chichewa and continued by asking

71

her name, age and what standard (grade) she was in. She replied shyly with an even broader smile.

There was only a Malawian family of four who dined close by. When the father and I looked at one another, I could tell that he was amazed that I, as a white person, was even inside an African rest house, much less eating there. He greeted me first.

"Hello, *Achimwene* [Brother], he said pleasantly in English.

I answered, "Thank you!" which is customary, although in Chichewa [*Zikomo!*].

He smiled, then continued to chat with me in Chichewa. He and his family were from Zomba, the capital of Malawi. They were on their way to Lilongwe, (which later became the capital of Malawi because it is more centrally located), and he was on a business trip. He was dressed for the part, with a white shirt, dark tie, smart black slacks, polished black leather shoes and a matching black leather belt. His wife and the children were also finely dressed. Mr. Chitowe and the primary school teachers were the only middle-class Malawians in my village, so it was rare to see other middle-class Malawians except in the big cities. We chatted for ten minutes, whereupon he complimented me on my Chichewa. I was making progress with that beautiful language. What was so encouraging was that Malawians were always kind and patient to bother to correct my mistakes which obviously helped me to improve my learning that much more rapidly.

Shortly thereafter I retired to my *tiny* room. The mud brick walls had not been plastered so they were dark brown, as was the dried mud floor. The mattress was very thin and lumpy, only eighteen inches wide, and not quite long enough for my 5'6" frame. The good news was that there were no bedbugs, which were notoriously pervasive in most Malawian rest houses. The room was windowless. The only light was provided by a single old petroleum jar half-filled with kerosene and a wick, the standard lamp in most Malawian villages.

Party On!

There was a soft knock at the door. When I opened it, a darling, shy, fifteen-year-old-girl asked if she could come in. She was apparently on the cusp of beginning her career as a prostitute. Although never known as a prude, I just could not bed her. Painfully disappointed, I barely heard her wistful half-whisper *"Ndapita tsopano"* [Goodbye now] as she slipped out of the room.

Next came a visit from the owner of the rest house, who tried in vain to convince me to provide work for this youngster. He even lowered the price from one dollar to fifty cents. I still couldn't do it. He and I did have an engaging conversation in English initially, for he wanted to practice his second language. Since I was just as eager to learn more Chichewa, we compromised: He spoke my language, and I, his. It was a pleasant encounter, although he, too, was obviously sorely disappointed that I wouldn't allow the girl to spend the night with me.

In spite of the uncomfortable mattress, I slept soundly throughout the night.

Village elders holding a trial.

VIOLATED!

"Music ... can name the unnamable and communicate the unknowable."

Leonard Bernstein

When I returned home the next day, my houseboy, Sami, was acting a bit strangely. When I asked in Chichewa, "What's going on?" he responded sheepishly.

"*Anthu akuba anabwera.*" (That means thieves had come by.) I thought that he'd said "*Anthu* akuda *anabwera:*" Africans came by (to visit).

I said, "Africans? Who were they?"

He said that he didn't know, squirming uneasily.

As I entered my hut, reality kicked me in the gut. My bed had been stripped and my footlocker emptied—and my paraffin (kerosene) lamp was missing. When I went out back to check out my kitchen, which was in a small, round, separate, small building, I noticed that my paraffin stove and all my pots and pans were gone, too.

What a violation! The chief was visibly upset, as were all my neighbors. They were embarrassed. Although most villagers had next to nothing, they collectively let me borrow enough "stuff" to sleep on and to cook with.

Sami was only nineteen. He had asked me for a job because my first houseboy, Adamu, had mouthed off one night after getting drunk that I was not enamored with his work. The latter was decidedly an understatement. Adamu could not do *any* of his expected duties

75

satisfactorily—cooking, cleaning, washing dishes—and especially simply looking after my dwelling. The most egregious example was when my two goats were stolen on his watch. (I found out later that he had abetted that transaction while I was in Blantyre recording *Sambani M'manja Mwanu Pochokera ku Chimbudzi* [Wash Your Hands After Going to the Latrine].)

Three months after my arrival in Nsiyaludzu Village, when I made the transition from my temporary digs in the abandoned storefront home to my newly constructed hut, I dismissed Adamu and took on Sami as my new houseboy. Sami performed better than Adamu, but not by much—at first. At least he could clean my hut and its surroundings. Initially, his cooking was abysmal, then suddenly it improved immeasurably. Later I learned that he secretively paid an elder neighbor woman to prepare my spartan meals. Clever, indeed.

Sami's flower gardening was an unexpected bonus—all my neighbors began planting beautifying flowers in their front yards. And when he suggested that he whitewash my hut's exterior, all the surrounding huts became whitewashed. This gave new meaning to "Keeping up with (the) Jack." It didn't take long for Nsiyaludzu to become the most beautiful village within miles, with the added flowers and whitewashed huts, complete with more improved latrines and a few more soak pits (to help control the mosquito menace). Peace Corps staff had encouraged us to "live by example," which was slowly coming to fruition in my village. This was most gratifying to me, and my neighbors seemed to be enjoying the changes, as well. The bad news is that the goats in the village readily ate *all* the flowers.

Sami was quite shy. He never spoke unless spoken to first. I honestly found it hard to bond with Sami. He was bright yet not well educated. Rumor had it that Sami was a superb soccer player, although I never got to see him on the pitch. He was a handsome, muscular, fit young man with a perpetual smile. He was also punctual, an unusual Malawian trait.

Violated!

After my first month working in my baby clinic, I invited Sami to replace the first chap I'd enlisted as an interpreter. The Peace Corps supervising physician had provided us with a long, exhaustive list in both English and Chichewa of questions and probable answers to facilitate our obtaining a detailed history on each child from its mother. However, because of so much repetition, it took me only a few weeks to ask, receive and respond to these interchanges with confidence. And whenever I encountered a complicated patient, I would consult immediately with Mr. Chitowe. Four months after my arrival, I decided to run my clinic without an interpreter. Sami was visibly disappointed because he lost that additional income.

Shortly after my return from the holiday party in Mzuzu, I received a note from the PC office in Blantyre that an American evaluator and his "new bride" were coming to make sure that this new Peace Corps project was being implemented properly. It turned out this chap was Calvin ("Bud") Trillin, a fledging writer. (A few years later I reminisced as I became familiar with his work in *The New Yorker*.)

The day of their arrival I was holding my weekly under-fives' baby clinic which was in the rear of the medical dispensary. The room was quite small. Only a curtain separated my room from that of Clementi, an elder chap in charge of wound care management. Experience had been an excellent teacher, for Clementi was quite skilled in dealing with complicated wounds as well as their associated dressings.

My examination room contained a small exam table for pediatric patients aged from birth to five years; a scale for weighing babies (but not one for the older kids); a very small kerosene stove and a small pot for sterilizing needles and glass syringes; and two chairs— one for the child's mother, the other for me.

Every Wednesday my clinic started at 8:00 a.m., and lasted until 6:00 or 6:30 p.m., when it became too dark to carry on. There was neither electricity nor kerosene lamps anywhere in the clinic. Mommas would bring in their infants, toddlers and other kids for their immunizations. I would give them advice about what to feed their children beyond breast milk and how to boil and store drinking water. Before leaving the clinic, I would set up a date for me to do a home visit to perform a cooking demonstration. The goal was to get them to add the flour of pounded up peanuts (groundnuts to the Brits) and a smashed cherry tomato to the child's maize porridge to get more protein and vitamin C in their diet.

As fate would have it, that clinic day was more hectic and crowded than usual, compounded by the disruption of our guests, who were, quite frankly, very much in the way. Bud had a clipboard with pages of evaluation forms and checklists. I was so busy with my routine of interviewing mothers about their children's health and needs and then following through with my examination, immunizations, instructions and follow-up information that I didn't have time to pay much attention to him, unless he asked a clarifying question.

Alice was not an official evaluator. She had begun the morning observing Mr. Chitowe's overrun clinic on the front side of the building but joined me and Bud after only ten minutes. I could tell that she was having a tough time adjusting to the crowding, the plethora of suffering patients, the unpleasant odors, the omnipresent flies, the relentless heat, the abject poverty and so many crying babies. Alice was experiencing full blown culture shock.

I pressed on seeing patients until noon. We then took a break for lunch, which provided me with a much-needed respite from the added stress of operating my clinic "under evaluation" in such a confining space. Because my hut was only 10 ft. x 14 ft., we had our meal outdoors: goat stew, *nsima*, rice, curried turnip greens and bottles of warm soda.

Lunch did provide an opportunity for me to get to know the Trillins better. Bud was balding, possessed a dry, quick wit, and liked to tell stories. He was not a particularly handsome man. I learned that he was beginning his fourth year with *The New Yorker* magazine, but that money was tight. Bud and Alice had only been married for a year-and-a-half, and because they had not been able to afford what he termed a proper honeymoon, he had convinced Alice that this short gig as a Peace Corps evaluator would provide that coveted delayed honeymoon as well as some welcomed financial relief.

Alice was blond, fair and attractive. How Bud had snagged her was remarkable to me. She was also shy. Alice was just telling me that she was interested in becoming an educator and possibly a writer, as Bud had encouraged her to do, when a large, loud crowd began to wend its way from the main (dirt) road a quarter-mile down the village path toward us.

Even before the enlarging angry throng reached my hut, I was totally undone by what I saw. Sami had been tied with twine around his arms and wrists so tightly that all four sites were bleeding. Moreover, what was even worse was that there was a similar string around his penis, and he was being led through the village literally in tow.

Culturally, Malawians are much more stoic about enduring pain than Americans or Europeans; therefore, I was moved by the tears flowing down Sami's face. I begged the leaders to please untie Sami. Initially they politely, yet firmly, disagreed. After a protracted dialog, the compromise was to at least release his penis.

Bud and Alice Trillin were in an obvious state of disbelief. Alice became ashen and remained totally silent throughout the four-hour ordeal. Bud frowned, squinted and simply shook his head. I requested that someone please ride their bicycle the seven miles south to the post office in Balaka to telephone the police in Ntcheu which was twenty-five miles to the north. Our village was just over the line into the Central Region, and not under the jurisdiction of the police unit in Balaka, which was in the Southern Region. There's nothing like bureaucracy to impede getting things done with dispatch.

When two police officers finally arrived, it was after 5:00 p.m. Mr. Chitowe had long since returned to resume taking care of the patients in his packed clinic. He had also graciously agreed to dismiss the mothers and their children waiting outside my clinic with the promise that I would provide an unscheduled make-up clinic the next morning.

The officer in charge deferred to me because the village leaders had referred to me as "the white doctor." He began by asking in English, "Sir, please tell me what this is all about?"

I quickly responded, "I will do so, sir, if you will please remove the string from this man's arms and wrists."

At first the village leaders continued their protestations—that is until I tactfully suggested that Sami be handcuffed as soon as the strings were removed. The eventual compromise was that Sami's ankles were shackled after the handcuffs had been applied.

The dialog with the police, the village people and me seemed to go on *ad infinitum*. I observed that Bud and Alice were drained emotionally. I asked the police to excuse me for a moment so that I could briefly explain to my guests that my afternoon clinic session had been postponed until the next morning, if their work was not done.

Bud responded wearily. "Jack, I'm amazed at what you are doing here, and your involvement today was extraordinary. You are one patient man, and it's obvious that the people value your being here."

"Thank you for your kind words. I just hope you got enough information to complete your evaluation."

"Fear not. Your clinic is *incredible*. I'm just grateful that the people around here are so protective of you."

Bud went on, mentioning that although the conditions were tough, I was obviously making a substantial contribution. By then I was hoping that he would stop talking and just take their leave. He finally did, saying, "Alice joins me in thanking you for your hospitality. We'll be moving on now for the rest house in Dedza." Alice managed a shy grin, then suddenly gave me a tight hug as she began to weep softly.

It was a most trying day for us *all*, especially for Sami. The additional issue for me was that the police officers still had more questions for the obligatory bureaucratic forms that needed to be filled out.

Three days later a police Land Rover unexpectedly delivered all my missing articles to my hut! People in the next village had noticed that some of my clothes had been hanging out to dry, and when they approached the hut, a strange man was using my frying pan to cook over an open fire. I was told that this chap had recently been released from prison, having served time for burglary. He had apparently convinced Sami to facilitate his wiping me out. The police had arrested him yet again, along with Sami.

Sami spent a year in prison. Not long after his release we bumped into each other at the market in Blantyre. When our eyes met, he quickly ran away, ignoring my pleading for us to chat.

Sami was lost in the crowd, forever.

Green Mamba

SNAKES

"One good thing about music, when it hits you, you feel no pain."

Bob Marley

Black Mamba: Juanita Maria Fuentes, a first-generation Cuban-American from Miami, was a member of the Tuberculosis (TB) Project Team which had arrived in Malawi three months before our public health group. Juanita Maria preferred to be called J.M.; however, since Malawians had difficulty saying that, they referred to her simply as "Jim," which obviously sounded masculine. It was a fitting nickname for this young woman, though, for she appeared more masculine than feminine.

J.M. lived and worked in Thyolo (pronounced CHO-lo), which is located in the Shire Highlands twenty-five miles east of Limbe, the Siamese twin city of Blantyre. The town and the district are famous for their tea plantations. The rolling hills are lush with beautiful bright green tea plants that spread eastward through Mulanje District and the tallest mountain in Malawi, Mt. Mulanje, at 10,000 feet. The area weather is on the cool side of sub-tropical.

She was on her motorcycle out in the bush late one afternoon on her way to follow up with some of her patients. As she grappled to keep the slow-moving bike on the rocky path, she thought she saw a tree limb out of the corner of her eye. Suddenly she realized that she wasn't under a tree. When she jerked her head to the right, she was staring into the menacing mouth of a big black snake!

In a reflexive panic, the young woman dove onto the ground immediately to her left. The snake struck as she fell, plunging its fangs deeply into her right calf.

The motorcycle's engine was still running and in gear. The snake was drawn to the glinting sun that was being reflected off the rotating chrome rim, and it began to strike rapidly and rhythmically at the back tire as it coiled its slithering body around her leg.

J.M. began shouting, *"Ndithandizeni!"* [Help me!] An African farmer who was returning from his garden responded. Fortunately, he had his hoe with him. And although most Malawians are deathly afraid of snakes, this man did not hesitate in quickly killing this one.

In Chichewa, J.M. asked, "How far is the local medical dispensary?" She hadn't known because she was headed in a different direction to make three house calls.

The farmer was sincere in his reply. "Madam, it's a mile away. I shall take you, please."

Malawians are very polite, for they've received a double dose of politeness—culturally, which is truly profound—*and* they had been colonized by the British. The farmer was about five feet tall and weighed a whopping one hundred pounds. The PCV weighed in at one hundred and sixty and was 5'7". He struggled to help her up to a standing position, hoisted her onto his back and walked as rapidly as he could to the dispensary without stopping to rest.

It was later confirmed that the snake was indeed a deadly black mamba. It measured eight feet long.

The lore associated the black mamba is legendary in Malawi with attributes such as magical, shrewd, intelligent, super-fast and most deadly at the top of the list. Its venom is highly toxic; reportedly the venom from one snake could kill over a dozen people. Black mambas get their name from the color inside their mouth. Their bodies tend to be gray or olive in color, although the snake that bit J.M. was *black*. Green mambas are smaller, slower and less venomous, yet deadly. Their lore includes being shy and elusive, tending to prefer to ambush their prey. They are a vivid bright green. Both snakes are feared universally.

So how did she survive?

Miraculously. That particular rural clinic had two things that almost all similar facilities did not: a kerosene-powered fridge and snake antivenin. My dispensary had neither. Yet another stroke of fate was that the medical assistant on duty was still there, completing paperwork. As soon as he had quickly taken her medical history, by protocol he didn't waste a moment in injecting two vials of the antidote: one vial in a circular manner around the fang wounds and the other deep within the thigh above the snakebite.

The medical dispensary where she had been taken was laid out the same as the one where Mr. Chitowe and I worked. These clinic facilities were cookie-cutter buildings over the entire country as a governmental cost-saving measure. It was just utilized differently because of the small fridge. Additionally, in the area where my clinic was held had previously been used for storage—pharmaceuticals, bandages, gauzes, tapes, a few linens and other essentials.

And how did we meet? By chance. A few months after her incident, J.M. and I met at the market near my village. I had gone there to shop for fresh vegetables. She had stopped for a soda. I had not expected to meet another white person there, although we do tend to stand out in a sea of black faces. I had heard her motorcycle arrive as I was walking up the hill from my hut. I found out a bit later that she was on her way to visit two women PCVs in the TB project who lived twenty-five miles north of me. Although we were meeting for the first time, she was quite friendly and loquacious.

"Are you in the baby clinic group?" she inquired in an amiable manner.

"Yes. Our dispensary is located down the hill and to the left, almost a half-mile from here," I responded.

After we had introduced ourselves, it dawned on me that she was the PCV who had been bitten by the black mamba, for news of it got around quickly—on MBC (Malawi Broadcast Company), in national newspapers and by word of mouth. She, in turn, was delighted to meet the person she called "the PCV rock star."

"You have become quite famous here in Malawi, Jack! Your songs are played incessantly on the radio," she said with sincere enthusiasm. "What's your next song going to be? Our project could use a song about tuberculosis."

"You're not going to believe this, J.M., but just yesterday I wrote a song about TB. I just don't know when I'll get to record it."

J.M. asked me to sing it to her. I demurred, letting her know that I didn't like singing *a cappella*. But she insisted that I share the Chichewa words with her, which I did. The gist of the song is to be aware of what TB is, how dangerous it can be, and to seek medical attention quickly at the hospital if symptoms of this disease become apparent. She was quite pleased that I had honored her project with such a promising, purposeful song.

Then I asked her about her encounter with the black mamba. J.M. shared the entire ordeal, including her hospital stay and the three surgical debridement procedures she had undergone. The scar on her calf was hideous. It measured 4 x 5 inches, was deeply disfiguring and was still very red. Yuk!

We found warm orange sodas at the market which we drank as we finished our conversation. J.M. was a dedicated volunteer. She could have resigned and returned home after her spectacular injury, but she would have no word of it. She returned to work just as soon as she could.

When J.M. had been transported from the dispensary by ambulance to Queen Elizabeth Hospital in Blantyre, the dead black mamba was also picked up and taken with her. A taxidermist was enlisted to preserve it, and that snake along with explanatory commentary resided on display in the Museum of Malawi for many years thereafter.

Green Mamba: Closer to home, one of our major community development projects in Nsiyaludzu Village was protecting a local spring in order to provide clean, fresh, safe water for all the surrounding villages. Mr. Chitowe and I borrowed a brick-making machine from its inventor, a Catholic priest who lived a hundred and fifty miles away. The transfer arrangements for the device had been facilitated by the Ministry of Health headquarters in Blantyre.

The ingenious concept involved precisely mixing anthill sand with fine sand from the dry riverbed [*dhambo*], watering down the concoction overnight, and then making large *hard* bricks in the press, without the need of a kiln for curing them. All that was required was an external skim of cement to protect the structure; none was needed between the bricks.

Nsiyaludzu was basically flat, with a gentle downslope from the main road heading westward. That same slope was exaggerated the more northwesterly one traveled through the village. That's the route from the dispensary to the construction site for the new protected water supply. It was the dry season again—hot and arid, similar to where I was from in south central Florida, yet without any nearby lakes.

The village men with whom I worked that day to transport our bricks from the dispensary to the construction site were Chalosi [Charles], Stefeni [Steven] and Faledi [Fred]. All four of us were dressed in shorts and ragged tee shirts. I was the only one wearing shoes. Stefeni, the most gregarious of our troupe, started the challenge in Chichewa: "I can carry more bricks at one time than you three," he boasted in a pseudo-haughty manner.

Chalosi countered in British-tinged Chichewa, "I can carry *more*, both at one time *and* overall," he said confidently.

I added, "I will carry more at one time, and overall *and* the fastest. You won't be able to keep up with me!"

"The losers must buy the others a gourd of *mowa* [beer] at Adekesa's bar," declared Faledi. The other three of us argued briefly for two gourds as the prize for the winner but backed off when Chalosi admitted he couldn't even cover three gourds if he were to lose.

Stefeni shouted, "Let the contest begin!"

Once the men from the village and I had made the requisite number of bricks to protect the spring, the bricks needed to be carried by hand the quarter mile from the clinic to the construction site. That's when the competition really began. I loaded up with six bricks and labored to make it to the spring without resting. The other three men behind me had seven bricks. I took eight on my next pass and waddled slowly down the path.

About a hundred yards from the clinic I heard the men frantically shout, "Aphiri!" (ah-PEE-rree), which was my Malawian clan name. "Njoka! Njoka!" (n-JOE-kah) means snake. I'd hoped that they were joking with me (pardon the puny pun), so I turned around awkwardly to look behind me: a long bright green snake was quickly closing in on me. I panicked!

In my fright I didn't think to use the eight bricks as weapons. Instead, I hastily dropped them and made a frantic dash for the spring. When I got there, I hurriedly grabbed two fistfuls of rocks and fired them onto the path behind me. Luckily for me, the snake was not there. Perhaps, when I had dropped the bricks, the creature had been scared off. Chalosi, Stefeni and Faledi, however, laughed their butts off at my frightened reaction to running away from what I, and they, were convinced was a green mamba—a dreaded, deadly, poisonous snake.

Before leaving for Peace Corps training, I'd read a magazine article about a Southern Rhodesian who had attempted to run his

Land Rover over a black mamba which had been stretched across the dirt road. The snake reared straight up quickly to avoid being hit, yet followed the vehicle for over twenty miles. As the driver was unloading his groceries, the mamba arrived and bit him. The chap died a few hours later.

That story had stuck in my mind—which explains why I was so afraid.

Medevac airlift

STUPID, STUPID, STUPID

*"Music expresses that which cannot be said and
on which it is impossible to be silent."*

Victor Hugo

Sometimes PCVs do some of the stupidest things:

Mike Davis was the most affable PC trainee. An Irish American Catholic, he was friendly, forgiving and forthright. Other "F" words to describe Mike also come to mind: funny, foxy and frisky. *Everyone* liked Mike.

The only time we spent some time together was in Nairobi, Kenya, the night before we departed for Malawi. Agreeing that we didn't really know each other that well, we chose to go to a nice bar for a few drinks. He was beginning to share his background with me when a cute young Kenyan woman overheard "Peace Corps"—Mike was telling me why he had joined. She politely interrupted, telling us that she had been taught by PCVs during secondary school, claiming that they were her best teachers *ever.* They started to chat with each other in earnest, and after about fifteen minutes I had to relieve myself. When I returned, they were gone. I hung around for one more drink before returning to the hotel.

The next morning, we had to be on the prearranged bus to the airport at 10:00 for our scheduled flight from Nairobi to Blantyre. When the head count was taken, Mike was the only absentee.

Our PC rep was shaken. She asked who had seen him last. Although I was reluctant to say anything and was on the cusp of doing so, Mike pulled up in a taxi, ten minutes late. When he got on the bus, everyone laughed and poked fun at him: "Where were you last night? Did you have fun? Were you with anyone we know? Don't tell us you got lost!" The volunteers were having fun. The staff members were pissed.

Mike sat down next to me. He looked as if he hadn't slept: He was disheveled, hair uncombed and unshaven. Mike winked at me and said that he would fill me in later. When we got to the airport we dallied going through immigration and customs so we could chat briefly.

"Sorry that I disappeared last night. Kalea invited me to go home with her."

I looked at him sideways. "You had just met her. What happened when I left you two for only a few minutes?" I was really curious to know.

"Well, I found out that she was a hooker. For a moment I was shocked, especially in the context of the Peace Corps for both of us. Then I felt the need to take her up on her offer," he said casually.

I jabbed him in the ribs. "Mike, you Catholic guys are so hypocritical! Don't you feel guilty?"

A gleam appeared in his bloodshot eyes. "That's what confession is all about." I didn't know whether to take him seriously. We both said no more.

Mike was stationed in Ntchisi, where he had set up an under-fives clinic. One Friday he rode his motorcycle to pick up his good friend, the headmaster of the local primary school. They went to a bar to drink beer together. Each imbibed quite a tally and both were drunk by the time they left.

It was raining heavily. As Mike turned into the headmaster's pathway, the motorcycle slid down in the mud. Mike's head hit a rock, and he was knocked out completely. The problem was that Mike had let the headmaster use his helmet. He obviously should not have allowed *anyone* to ride on his motorcycle without wearing a helmet. Mike had suffered a depressed skull fracture and was not arousable.

The ensuing logistics were complicated and difficult to arrange. It wasn't easy to get Mike into the headmaster's house because the headmaster was fall-down drunk in the mud. It took his wife and two of their neighbors to get Mike out of the rain and mud into their home. Notifying the PC office had to be done through a trunk telephone line at the local post office; that was eventually accomplished by a teacher from the primary school once he had been tracked down by the headmaster's wife. Dispatching an ambulance to have Mike brought to Queen Elizabeth Hospital in Blantyre took an inordinate amount of time. Arranging for Mike to receive appropriate treatment without neurosurgical care in Malawi was daunting.

The PC Director in Blantyre telephoned Peace Corps headquarters in Washington, DC. Subsequently, after a bureaucratic harangue of deciding which agency was going to pay for this emergency venture, a U.S. Air Force medical C-131 was finally dispatched from Germany to Blantyre. It was no easy task to arrange for an ambulance to take Mike and the Air Force personnel in a timely fashion from Queen Elizabeth Hospital to Chileka Airport. Then the air traffic control delay for take-off was inexplicable.

Once the plane was at a smooth cruising altitude, Mike was operated upon by two Air Force neurosurgeons to lift the depressed skull fragment off his injured brain. This didn't transpire until five days after his mishap. Mike remained unconscious.

In Germany, after he was stable postoperatively, Mike was airlifted back to the States. He was eventually sent to a public health hospital on Long Island, New York, for "rehabilitation," although he remained in a coma for *years*.

Then one fine day he woke up, smiled and announced, "Hey, I'm hungry!" Then he cried out, "Why can't I move my legs?" Mike was a paraplegic.

He was immediately entered into an extensive rehab program in order to regain his upper body strength. Once he was fit to leave the hospital, he was hired as an assistant desk officer by the Peace Corps, where he helped to coordinate PC programs all over the continent of Africa. Mike worked there for three years before his untimely death.

John Strain was handsome. All the women trainees agreed, and most of the men in our group did, too. He was from California, had attended university in the state of Washington and was blessed with a winning smile, sandy blond hair, an athletic physique and a positive attitude. John had a tremendous work ethic which earned him the enviable reputation of being an outstanding Peace Corps Volunteer.

Yes, John was indeed handsome, for it was apparently the deciding factor in his being chosen to represent being the three-hundredth PCV to serve in Malawi. That meant that when our group of thirty volunteers landed in Blantyre, the PC/Malawi office had arranged for John to be interviewed and photographed by the leading newspapers in Malawi as well as interviewed by the sole radio station. He handled those responsibilities quite admirably and with aplomb.

John was the chap who was in the lorry with me when I was dropped off in my village. After his first year in Malawi, he had been visited by his wealthy godmother from California, who had invited him to join her on a vacation to Kenya, Tanzania and Madagascar. At Chileka Airport near Blantyre, just before their flight departed for Nairobi, Kenya, John impulsively pulled a government-issued poster off the wall that condemned mini-skirts (a pet peeve of President Banda).

John returned to his post after a marvelous month-long holiday. It wasn't until six weeks later that he was arrested for defiling government property and forced to leave the country immediately.

Once John returned to the States after having served half of his planned two-year tour with the Peace Corps, he worked for a bank for eight months before deciding to procure an MBA through the prestigious Executive Education Program within the Thunderbird School of Global Management at Arizona State University. He then enjoyed a distinguished career in the banking industry for many years.

John's downfall was a combination of poor financial decisions and far too much alcohol. Although John did not do so in training or in Malawi, he drank excessively after leaving Malawi and for many ensuing years. The booze eventually ruined his marriage, strained his relationship with his two grown children, and diminished his professional standing. The latter caused him to struggle financially. His good looks also went to seed, so much so that many former PCVs didn't recognize him at the fortieth-year reunion of our reporting to PC training, the main detraction being his excess weight. To his credit, John remained intimately involved with the Malawi XI group. He actually became our *de facto* leader by helping to plan our reunions and keeping all of our contact information up to date through his computer wizardry. John was the focal point of keeping our group intact. Many of us wondered if his drinking was directly connected with his having been thrown out of Malawi, although no one wanted to broach the proverbial elephant in the room.

I, too, was guilty of stupidity.

"May I help you, sir?" a Malawian in his mid-fifties implored, in English.

"Yes, please, sir," I moaned. Then without hesitating I asked, "Do you have any soap and water so that I may clean up my wounds?" I had learned in PC training that my wounds needed immediate attention.

"Absolutely. Please allow me to help you to my house. I'll bring your bag and your *mtututu* [motorcycle] once you're inside," he offered graciously.

How did I meet Arthur?

Having been invited to go on a mini-vacation to Quelimane, Mozambique, with two of my PCV male friends and a British female PC staff member, I headed out on my motorcycle for the hundred-mile trek to meet up with them in Blantyre. My only suitcase was a hard-shelled two-suiter which I couldn't fit on the bike. I "solved" that problem by taking off my belt, looping it through the handle and putting my neck through the belt. However, that left the suitcase unanchored precariously on the back seat.

About halfway to Blantyre I was jolted by a stretch of washboard corrugations on the dirt road. Abruptly, the heavy suitcase slipped off to the side, and I fell off the bike straight away. Dazed, I was startled to hear Arthur's voice offering to help me.

My only obvious injuries were nasty, dirty cuts on both palms. Getting those wounds cleaned up was *pain*fully time-consuming. As painful as the scrubbing went, I made sure to remove all the sand and grit; otherwise, the debris would have left me with gross, unwanted "tattoos."

I was impressed with the Malawian gentleman who had come to my rescue. Arthur Gondwe, nearing retirement as a mid-level bank manager in Zomba, was presently home on a two-week vacation.

Mr. Gondwe was most gracious to me. He made sure that I had enough hot, fresh, clean water and soap for cleansing the wounds on my hands. Then he dressed them meticulously with gauze and tape from the only medicine cabinet I'd seen in a Malawian home, including Mr. Chitowe's.

He was also a pleasant conversationalist. As I scrubbed and soaked my wounds, we chatted about a recent incident in which some dissident rebels had been ambushed and subsequently killed when they had tried to re-enter the country while President Banda was on a diplomatic visit with President Johnson in Washington, DC. He also introduced me to his lovely wife, Roseby, who insisted on having me stay for lunch. This couple was a perfect representation of Malawian culture—warm, welcoming and giving. I was most appreciative of their generous hospitality, and I couldn't thank them enough.

I was reluctant to leave. My wounds were beginning to become more painful, and the Gondwes didn't have any aspirin or any other analgesics. I dreaded getting back on the motorcycle for I knew that the washboard road would exacerbate the pain in my aching hands.

Mr. Gondwe was incredibly helpful in making sure that my suitcase was as secure as possible in being attached to my back. He had found some strips of rubber from an old inner tube in his workshop that he fastened to me, the suitcase and the cycle. His clever jerry-rigging definitely got me to Blantyre without further incident.

The old adage is true, indeed: "There ain't no cure for stupid!"

Playing with Achitowe's son, Jemosi [James], during a break
outside my baby clinic where he was a patient.

THE ART OF MEDICINE

*"I think music in itself is healing. It's an explosive expression
of humanity. It's something we are all touched by.
No matter what culture we're from, everyone loves music."*

Billy Joel

I was immersed in seeing countless patients in my baby clinic when I was politely interrupted by Mr. Chitowe, who requested an emergent consultation.

"Jack, I have a most interesting patient to share with you."

I complied immediately because, as the medical expert and leader of the dispensary, it was so rare for him to involve me in his clinical machinations. He filled me in a bit as we walked around the outside of the building.

"A woman has refused to be seen by me, demanding to be evaluated by the white doctor," he explained. "She claims that there's a snake in her vagina."

I was stunned. "So, what am I supposed to do, Mr. Chitowe? I may be white, but I'm no doctor, as you well know, sir."

"Please perform a basic pelvic exam on her, if you will. Otherwise, I won't be able to continue to see the remainder of the patients waiting in my clinic."

"But I've never done a pelvic before!" After a brief pause, I tried a bit of nervous humor. "The are only two things I know about a vagina—it is warm, and it is moist."

Mr. Chitowe smiled faintly and guided me into his side of the dispensary.

My paltry "paramedic" training was based upon discerning whether children were well or ill. In PC training we had been taught that ill children were *not* to be inoculated. Period. Only well children were to receive the immunizations I provided: DPT routinely, measles occasionally and smallpox infrequently, based on what was available through the Ministry of Health.

The consult involved a thirty-year-old woman who had been awakened the night before when she had felt a snake crawl into her vagina. Today she had walked three miles to have it removed. The woman insisted vehemently that I be the one to extract it. Mr. Chitowe obviously wanted off the hook.

After procuring a kerosene lamp from his home next door and clearing a space in the dispensary's closet where he kept his medicines, Mr. Chitowe asked the patient to disrobe and to lie down on a sheet on the floor. Then I was invited to examine her. I was incredibly nervous. There was not a latex glove in the entire clinic; furthermore, there was neither an examination table with stirrups nor a speculum in order to get the job done properly. With Mr. Chitowe's guidance, I slowly examined the patient by parting her labia with both hands, then gently probed her vagina with the fingers of my right hand. I shared with both the patient and Mr. Chitowe that the snake was no longer present.

They were most appreciative. As I went to wash my hands, Mr. Chitowe filled out forms so that she could ride free on a bus to be further evaluated by Mr. C.'s boss, the principal medical assistant (PMA) at Ntcheu Regional Hospital, located twenty-five miles north of our facility.

That evening we met briefly after work. "I'm curious, Mr. Chitowe, why did you refer the patient to the PMA in Ntcheu?"

"Because we were not able to provide a proper female examination. The Ministry of Health guidelines require referral to the regional hospital for any clinical matters we can't handle," he answered, and went on to explain that her diagnosis involved at least three possibilities: a round worm had crawled out of her anus and entered her vagina, she had a psychiatric problem, or maybe even both. I was appreciative of his explanation. The question I was too embarrassed to ask was why he had invited me to perform an exam for which I was most definitely not qualified? Acquiescence to the patient's demand? Providing me with some additional clinical exposure? I'll never know.

What happened next was extraordinary, documented in a courtesy letter Mr. Chitowe received four days later from Ntcheu Regional Hospital in response to his referral: "The PMA received the patient graciously. He listened intently to her story, then had a nurse put her up in stirrups. He examined her vagina with a speculum and declared that he saw the snake. He then wrestled it from the deepest refuge of her birth canal, threw it to the floor, stomped on it until it was annihilated, called in a janitor to sweep it up and put it in the incinerator, and quietly informed the patient that she was cured. The woman was tremendously relieved and incredibly grateful."

My sarcastic comment to Mr. Chitowe was, "The PMA broke both of his arms patting himself on the back." Mr. C. laughed because he was familiar with the PMA's flowery English. I then asked, "What does Conversion Reaction mean, the final diagnosis that the PMA concluded?"

Mr. Chitowe responded, "It's a psychiatric diagnosis. Something to do with how a person copes with a problem. I'm confused because that diagnosis usually involves a pseudo-coma, blindness or some other neurologic symptom which this person did not have. Interesting. I'll have to ask the PMA the next time we see each other. Stop by my house tomorrow and let's look up conversion reaction together."

We did just that the next day. As I read that section in his medical textbook, I had to keep asking Mr. Chitowe to translate medical words and related terminology. And although Mr. C. had been correct in challenging the diagnosis of conversion reaction, I still had another question:

"Why did the PMA make a psychiatric diagnosis?"

"Remember, Jack, he did perform a pelvic exam which did not reveal a snake in her vagina. That's when he went through the necessary steps in our culture to cure her and relieve her obsession."

A week after returning to her village, the appreciative patient invited Mr. Chitowe and me to come to her home for a celebratory feast to honor us for relieving her misery and for saving her life. The poor woman had had a cow slaughtered and roasted and had paid a local brew-master to brew up a fifty-gallon drum of village beer. This party was more festive than any other I'd experienced in Malawi, whether with Americans, Malawians or both. I could feel the genuine excitement in that village, for our patient had been cured, and she and everyone else were most appreciative.

As the sun was beginning to set, a small bonfire was lit. I also finally learned the patient's name—Lovinesi Ulemu—although she preferred to be called by her *mfunda* [clan name], *Anachisale*.

While Mr. Chitowe and I each savored a gourd of *mowa* [village beer] while the villagers gathered for the feast, he observed, "What a lovely evening, Jack! These people are quite happy."

"I agree. I just hope that we don't drink too much so that we'll be able to ride our bicycles the three miles back home without crashing in the dark," I said. I was only half-kidding.

Anachisale approached us. It's customary for a woman to say *Odi* [May I come in / approach], or at least *Zikomo* [Thank you / pardon me], crouch on one or both knees, proffer her extended right arm while touching her right forearm with her left hand, shake hands with each guest, and finally say *Moni* [Hello] to each person separately. She was a gracious, polite host. Passing *moni* doesn't begin until guests are seated. Since Mr. Chitowe and I were provided the only two chairs in the village, the ceremony had begun.

Chief Salomoni greeted us warmly. He also squatted beside us as he, too, sipped *mowa*. After every adult had casually ambled over to greet us, it was around eight o'clock when the speeches began, starting with the chief. Anachisale delivered an impassioned oration which extolled the clinical prowess of Mr. Chitowe and me which contained *zikomo* [thank you] numerous times. When Mr. Chitowe was asked to speak, I realized that I would be next. I was always reluctant to speak Chichewa in front of Mr. Chitowe. His Chichewa was crisp and proper; mine was elementary and mistake ridden. I was more comfortable speaking Chichewa with villagers, for they were patient and forgiving of my errors. Tonight, I decided to relax and do my best in expressing my gratitude for such a wonderful, celebratory feast, and for Anachisale's having been cured. Each speech received an enthusiastic round of applause. We had so much fun!

We finally began enjoying the roasted beef around 9:30. The food was delicious and probably even more so because we were ravenously hungry by then. The revelry lasted well into the night.

As Mr. Chitowe and I slowly peddled our way back along the pathway to Nsiyaludzu Village, he waxed philosophic, "I love practicing medicine, Jack. I simply enjoy helping people get well." I listened to his dedication to his profession, marveled at how people in surrounding villages admired him, and reflected on what had transpired with Anachisale, from her presentation to our dispensary through tonight's celebration.

Although I quietly accepted all of this graciously, I had learned a tremendous lesson: the PMA had been masterful in knowing what that woman had needed and went about casting out the demon with true *professionalism*. And even though it was he who had cured her, I also learned that grace is something you receive when you don't deserve it.

As an avid observer and an equally eager participant, I was experiencing a plethora of raw clinical medicine in such an isolated rural medical dispensary! I had joined the Peace Corps in part to afford me the time to sort out whether I should become a physician or a pastor. I recalled how I had agonized over that decision during the time I was also not sure if the Peace Corps was going to be right for me. Now this unique series of experiences definitely helped me to decide unequivocally to apply to medical school and therefore forego seminary. What a relief! I was finally sure of what I wanted to pursue professionally.

Cover of the audiocassette version of "Ufa wa Mtedza"

The child I am holding, Elisabeti [Elizabeth], was diagnosed with marasmus (severe malnutrition) before we began feeding her peanut flour maize porridge.

#1 ON THE HIT PARADE

"The most exciting rhythms seem unexpected and complex,
the most beautiful melodies simple and inevitable."

W.H. Auden

How many people get to hear themselves sing on the radio? The first time I heard myself singing on MBC, I almost fell out of the barber's chair. I was getting a haircut near the market in Balaka, a town seven miles south of my village, when *Brush the Flies Outta Your Babies' Eyes* came blasting from the radio in a nearby shoe cobbler's stand. I was absolutely stunned! What was even more amazing was to hear it played again within fifteen minutes.

The barber commented to a small group of men waiting to be served in his tiny open-air shop. "I heard that song played at least six times yesterday. Who is that European singing with The Jazz Giants?"

A young man replied, "I think that his name is Jack *Chakuti* [Something]. Isn't he with the Peace Corps?"

I didn't say a word, although I did hear the DJ go on and on so fast that the only part I kept hearing repeated was "Jack Allison and The Jazz Giants." The rest was hard to make out. It was truly unreal to hear myself singing on the radio…and twice in one day! I thought to myself, "I wonder if this song will catch on? I've written one more, and I have others I'd like to pursue. This is truly amazing!"

So how did this all come about?

AFTER THE FIRST THREE MONTHS IN our villages with our newly constituted Public Health/Environmental Sanitation Project, the Peace Corps office in Blantyre arranged for our group to attend a debriefing conference at Cape Maclear, a small, quaint resort on beautiful Lake Malawi. I was definitely ready for a break and eager to reconnect with my friends from training. A nearby PCV and I were also eager to share our latest project with our PCV compadres, which was prompted by our observations.

Malawian mothers carry their babies on their back. Once the baby has suckled and has been changed, the mama will place the baby on her back, secure it with a large wraparound cloth to allow the baby to sleep as she goes about her work. We volunteers observed that when the baby was out of mama's line of sight, flies congregated on their infants' eyes. Then after the flies had subsequently visited with other babies, before long the entire village would come down with pink eye.

A week before the conference, I and my fellow volunteer, Jill McCoy, got together to make some educational posters for our baby clinics. She was posted in Balaka. Jill could draw exceptionally well, and I was blessed with decent penmanship. She drew two posters with a giant black fly on each, upon which I printed, in Chichewa, "Brush the flies outta your babies' eyes to prevent eye disease." These posters helped to spruce up our clinics, and they aided us in getting an important public health message across to mothers to help prevent pink eye from spreading throughout their villages.

At Cape Maclear I was enjoying my first tub bath since reporting to my village. I had filled the antique lion-clawed tub with *hot* water right up to my nose when the vision of the fly poster danced before my mind's eye on the ceiling above. Spontaneously I started putting the Chichewa words to an original tune. I dallied in the tub for a *long* time as I worked through the entire song.

Fearful of losing all the stuff going through my head—words, tune, intro, lead guitar, yackety sax, bass, drums—I jumped out of the bathtub and raced down to the beach (no, I wasn't naked!) to borrow a cassette player and an empty tape. The PCVs on the beach were curious to know where I had been, why I was late in joining everyone, and what I was so excited about. When I explained that I had written my first song, not one person shared my excitement—that is until a few weeks later, after I had recorded this song (*Pirikitsani Nchenche*) [Brush the Flies] with The Jazz Giants, the most popular African band in all of Malawi. It was aired quite frequently on MBC, the only radio station extant in the country, and it became an immediate success! Folks all over Malawi began sending in postcards for MBC's Request Night, asking that *Brush the Flies Outta Your Babies' Eyes*, by that crazy European, be dedicated to their sweethearts.

That was the first indication I had that a public health song could serve both educationally and as entertainment. People would spontaneously move rhythmically to my song, and others would flat-out dance to it. And please note that "crazy" was a term of endearment that was used frequently on those postcards. Additionally, anyone white in Malawi is referred to as a "European" no matter from whence they may have come.

WHAT HAPPENED NEXT WAS EVEN MORE pivotal in my nascent songwriting career. The day after returning to Nsiyaludzu Village, after recording "Brush the Flies," I wrote *Ufa wa Mtedza* [Peanut Flour], which became #1 on the Hit Parade in Malawi for the next three years. The gist of the translation is "Put pounded up peanut flour in your babies' maize porridge (we would say cornmeal mush in the South) and feed it to them three times a day if you want your children to be healthy" (to weigh a lot on the scale).

In today's parlance, *Ufa* went viral! Although "Brush the Flies" was a hit, *Ufa* was a mega-hit. Within six weeks, the Peace Corps office sent me a note, requesting that I be interviewed by *The Malawi Times* the next time I was in Blantyre. After that article appeared, two other reporters pestered the PC office until they acquiesced for me to be photographed for the front page of their respective newspapers, *Nyasa News,* and *Malawi Today*. That's when Lucius Chikuni, the founder of MBC, arranged for me to be featured on his popular, creative show, "Improving Your Health." Lucius and I became fast friends immediately.

When I was greeted by Lucius upon my arrival at MBC, I found him to be warm, affable, confident, and intelligent, all with more than a hint of American English. When I asked him about the latter, he replied, "Yes, I studied in the States for four years. I got a degree in communications with emphasis on radio and television production from the University of Missouri in Columbia."

"But there is not one television station in Malawi!" I said.

"Be patient, my man. There will be," he said. He certainly had me convinced. And he was correct, although it took many years for television to be introduced there.

Then he began the interview. "Jack, your songs are becoming quite popular here in Malawi. Why do you think that's so?"

"Lucius, I'm so glad they are popular, but I really can't say why. I can also say that my own sudden popularity is both satisfying because of my work in the village and a bit of an unexpected ego trip, as well, for now the messages of my songs are being shared with the entire nation several times a day. I honestly didn't expect people to embrace my music. What can I say? This adventure is meaningful to me and to my Peace Corps colleagues, and it's also a lot of fun!"

Lucius asked me about my goals. I explained that each song had at least one message that we were trying to get across and that my songs were also quite simple. I went on to add that my goal was to reinforce those basic messages with the hope of changing behaviors so that Malawians would become healthier.

Lucius continued. "I agree with you. Delivering health education messages via music is a unique approach. How did you come up with that idea?"

I explained how our Peace Corps physician, Dr. Lee Ellison, had encouraged me to write some jingles about our work and how that had evolved in spite of my initial hesitation because I was a singer, not a composer. It was the fly poster that ended up being the prompt that initiated my songwriting venture. Lucius chuckled when I reminded him that writing in Chichewa was easier than writing in English because all Chichewa words end in a vowel, making rhyming far easier.

Lucius interviewed me for an hour. He asked many questions about my songs. I could tell that he valued my innovative approach to health education for the masses, and he endorsed my music multiple times during our time on the air. The interview was a relaxed, engaging conversation. Lucius asked relevant questions which made me feel at ease—an interviewee is only as good as the interviewer.

Lucius was the consummate pro. Years later, he served as the Ambassador from Malawi to the U.S.A.

Me singing "Brush the Flies Outta Your Babies' Eyes"
on a store front "stage" in Nsanje, Malawi.

PLETHORA OF SONGS & JINGLES

"Music is the universal language of mankind."

Henry Wadsworth Longfellow

As a result of my newly found popularity, I became a celebrity. I was recognized everywhere I went. Many Malawians would approach me with, "Are you the one?" I was invited to sing spontaneously at nightclubs in Blantyre, the commercial capital of Malawi. Women—Malawian, American, British, Swedish, Canadian—were eager to dance with me and to chat and share a beer. What an unbelievable experience!

What I had not expected was how positive my newly found fame would be with the Peace Corps family. PCVs were quite gracious and supportive. Whenever I was in Blantyre, most often in conjunction with recording a new song or being interviewed for the radio or a newspaper, kudos abounded from them: "*Ufa wa Mtedza* is so popular in my area" or "I hear your songs on the radio all day and night" or "I'm using your songs in my baby clinic and during my cooking demonstrations" or "What's it like to be a star?"

I didn't have to say much for the answer to the latter was obvious. PC staff, especially "The Brass," treated me with a deference I had not anticipated, yet I accepted as graciously as I knew how. My music did wonders for improving Peace Corps' public relations with their Malawian counterparts and other government officials across the board.

EMBASSY OF THE
UNITED STATES OF AMERICA

Blantyre
May 7, 1968

Dear Jack,

My visit to Nsyaludzu is one of the richest experiences I have had in Malawi. It was rich because it exposed me to a lot of hard working, sincere, dedicated people who are trying, with the help of enthusiastic and talented young men like yourself, to improve their lot in this world and find a better life for their children.

It was inspiring — to see what good leaders — Malawian and American — black and white —

do when united in common against Africa's age old bitter enemies, ignorance, and disease.

Keep up the good fight. You make us all proud Americans.

Sincerely,

Marshall P. Jones
Ambassador

EMBASSY OF THE
UNITED STATES OF AMERICA

FETERE
TAMACHULUKITSA
ZOKOLOLA

BLANTYRE
11 JAN
10 MAY
1968
MALAWI

Mr Jack Allison
Peace Corps Volunteer
Nsyaludzu Village
Post office
Balaka

The U.S. ambassador to Malawi, Marshall Jones, even came to my village to pay me a visit. He was accompanied by the PC Director, Monroe McKay, affording them six hours of "windshield time," which our director especially appreciated. Ambassador Jones' visit was an honor for me and Mr. Chitowe. The ambassador was pleasantly surprised to learn about our manifold local community development projects when he had only expected to chat about the pop-

Ambassador Jones and me. I'm the one with the sugar cane on my shoulder.

ularity and potential impact of my music. The unfortunate downside was the ambassador's low-key refusal to visit other PCVs, for once word got out that he had visited with me, his office received numerous invitations from PCVs all over Malawi for him to visit and celebrate their own local improvement projects. His not doing so was damaging to his image among the entire American contingency in Malawi.

Mr. Chitowe and I took pride in touring the ambassador through the medical dispensary as a multitude of patients awaited our return to work. Jones was noticeably shaken by that teeming mass of humanity waiting to be seen and by the overall squalor in our village. He was eager to return to my hut for a few more words before returning to Blantyre. Once inside the relative comfort of my tiny swelling, he was visibly stunned when I casually mentioned what I had heard on the

113

Voice of America radio station while I was shaving early that morning: "Mr. Ambassador, I was shocked when President Johnson announced this morning on national news back home that he will not be running for re-election."

Jones had not heard the news. He became red-faced and quite fidgety, and asked me for more details. After I had added a few more nits and bits, he said that he needed to return to the embassy and departed abruptly. Being a political appointee by President Johnson left Jones uncertain about his own future in Malawi. His tenure ended up lasting another two years.

I was encouraged with the win-win aspects of incorporating my songs and jingles in my own clinic, especially during my cooking demonstrations. Although I have always eschewed singing *a cappella* (and I don't play the guitar), I felt comfortable singing to the mothers and children in the village because they seemed both mildly amused *and* clearly appreciative of my teaching. Performing in each village and briefly during each clinic was really enjoyable, for little girls *and* boys wanted to dance with me as I sang, which prompted mothers to dance among themselves. Somehow my songs connected with them, and I was so pumped *and* hopeful that my messages were not only being received but also acted upon positively.

I continued to write other health education songs and jingles which also became popular with Malawians:

• *Chiwewe* [Rabies] was played incessantly on MBC and ended up being the second most popular jingle of the sixteen that I recorded in Malawi. It implored people to have their dogs inoculated against this fatal disease, and this jingle was credited with getting rabies under far better measurable control during that time.

Others, with their English titles, included:

- *Wash Your Hands After Going to the Latrine* [This song became popular, for it reminded people that since they always wash their hands before eating, they need to do the same after using the latrine];
- *Boil Your Drinking Water* [Malawian mothers especially liked this tune, as it was dedicated to them];
- *TB Control* [The PC Tuberculosis Project Team appreciated this one];
- *Self-Help Schemes Help to Build the Country of Malawi* [This song was used for community development projects all over the country by many governmental and non-governmental agencies];
- *Make War on Ignorance, Poverty and Disease* [I got in trouble with this one! See the chapter on *John Tembo*];
- *The Best Foods for Our Children are a Mixture* [A song used to augment the message in *Ufa wa Mtedza*];
- *Safe Driving* [The first road safety song ever recorded in Malawi];
- *Bird Protection* [To remind people that birds eat the mosquitoes which cause malaria];
- *Crop Selection* [a song to bolster FMB, the Farmers' Marketing Board];
- *Blood Donation Song,* bilingually [Malawians were introduced to this life-saving campaign]; and
- *We Need to Take Good Care of Our Health,* which became the signature song for yet another popular radio health show hosted by Lucius Chikuni.

I became more and more passionate about my songs as I witnessed what was occurring around me. Gradually some babies gained weight and began to thrive after being introduced to *ufa wa mtedza* [peanut flour in their maize porridge]. However, it was slow going. Malnutrition was one of the many factors affecting survival of the babies in my clinic, including measles, pneumonia, diarrhea and a multitude of hard-hitting viruses, which also took their toll. Life is tough in Africa, especially for the young ones, yet I was excited about the overall change that was evolving. As I had shared with Lucius Chikuni, with MBC's "blaring" my songs and jingles many times each day, my health education messages were getting exposure with the masses. Every village had at least one radio therein, and it blasted forth from 7:00 a.m. until 6:00 p.m. daily, with quietude on most Sundays.

Popularity on a national scale is something I had to adjust to. I lived in the bush, so it was exceedingly rare that my work and my off-duty life were interrupted. However, when I went into Blantyre, or even spoke Chichewa while anywhere on the road, people would recognize me and want me to chat with them. Often strangers around me would start singing one of my songs. When I would playfully join in, the crowd would grow larger. This would last through at least two songs, but sometimes three or four. We would sing, dance a bit and clap our hands. The rhythm was infectious. I couldn't believe it! How much gratifying fun could one man have?

Wanting to test the record business in Malawi, a representative from Phillips Record Company in Holland approached me about allowing *Ufa wa Mtedza*, the Peanut Flour Song, as side-A on a 45-rpm record. (Remember the small disc with the large hole in the middle?) Astonishingly, it sold out, all 10,000 copies, within seven days—in the poorest country in the world! *And* I was undone when royalty checks came flooding in.

Since I was a Peace Corps Volunteer who was not allowed to pocket extra income, the Peace Corps office in Blantyre graciously helped me to set up a "mini-foundation" from which PCVs could access funds for local self-help projects. Cogent examples were providing money for building an addition to the library of a secondary school, buying much needed books to enhance those libraries and constructing latrines for a primary school.

London-based Grenada Television, Ltd., asked that I be featured on a private hour-long British documentary film on volunteerism in Africa. Representatives from Grenada had filmed a nurse, a teacher and a pharmacist—all Brits—yet they only had twenty minutes of usable footage. One rep kept hearing my songs being played quite frequently on MBC, and when she learned that I was a Peace Corps Volunteer *and* that my songs and jingles contained health education messages, she made her way to my village from Blantyre. She convinced me to be a part of their proposed documentary. Since my clinic space was too small to allow proper filming, we had to move my clinic outdoors. I also granted permission for *Ufa wa Mtedza* to be used as background music for my segment, yet I was not prepared when even more impressive royalty checks continued to arrive.

Shortly thereafter, there was a radio announcement on MBC, inviting songwriters to enter a national contest focused on extoling the merits of fertilizer. Because of the popularity of my songs and jingles, the repetitive questions I kept getting were "Are you going to enter the contest?" and "Have you written your song yet?" I decided to give it a shot. It didn't take me long to compose the words and music to this twenty-second jingle:

> "Fertilizer increases crop yields (X2). You will earn a lot of money. You will get a lot of food. Please buy fertilizer from FMB (Farmers' Marketing Board)." [*Feteleza achulukitsa zokolola* (X2). *Mudzapeza ndalama zambiri. Mudzapeza chakudya chambiri. Gulani feteleza ku FMB*].

The published rules were that the entry songs had to be prerecorded before the contest. MBC had the only recording studio in the entire country. The good news is that MBC did not charge for any of the recordings. The bad news is that my usual band for recording my songs,

The Jazz Giants, was away upcountry on a brief tour. That meant I had to find another band in short order.

After auditioning three bands over a weekend, the best of the lot was The Woodpeckers. The saving grace was their lead guitar player, Sydney. He and I worked diligently together with the other band members to rehearse the jingle *ad infinitum* to get it right.

The songs were played on MBC, one after the other, with typical commentary bantered by the DJ and the three judges. I had not expected the harshness of much of the judgments after each song was played, especially considering the usual ultra-politeness associated with Malawian culture.

My jingle was played third from the end of the contest, and the response was overwhelmingly positive, both by the crowd and by the judges. The DJ joined in, and in all fairness, the final two songs were played *pro forma*. My song came in first, and I was delighted! As with so many contests, no one recalls which ones came thereafter. The large cash prize, by Malawian standards, was deposited immediately into the mini-foundation. I was both amazed and pleased that I had won, especially without The Jazz Giants. It was the only song I ever did with The Woodpeckers. Because the Farmers' Marketing Board (FMB) was eager to promote fertilizer, *Feteleza* was played day and night, and became the third most popular song I recorded in Malawi.

Only twice in my three-year tour with Peace Corps/Malawi did a vehicle come to my village to hand-deliver a letter to me. The car arrived at my hut while I was completing some obligatory paperwork for both the Ministry of Health and the Peace Corps. The driver presented me with an invitation to attend an important upcoming meeting at the corporate offices of Mobil Petroleum, Ltd., (Malawi), in Blantyre. Because of my clinic schedule and prior scheduled follow-up visits and cooking demonstrations in surrounding villages, I was not able to comply for a week. A private car was sent to pick me up.

Once in Blantyre, I was warmly welcomed by the British managing director of the company. "Good afternoon, Mr. Allison. We are so happy that you have agreed to meet with us." After a few more pleasantries, he cut to the chase. "Shell Oil recently commissioned a jingle, in English, which touts their petrol. Since we've been politely reminded by members of our own Malawian staff that Malawians also purchase petrol, we would like to ask you to please consider writing a bilingual jingle that extols the virtues of Mobil petrol."

"How much did Shell pay?" I inquired.

"X amount."

I countered. "Make it $3X$, and I'll do it."

I should have asked for more. Indeed, I was paid handsomely for that project, the highest ever for a similar jingle in Malawi.

Lorry on the Great North Road from Kapiri Mposhi, Zambia
to Dar es Salaam, Tanzania

MT. KILIMANJARO

"Music can change the world because it can change people."

Bono

When I picked up my mail in early September of my first year in Malawi, the letter I received from Bill Schmidt, my buddy in Ntchisi, quickly caught my eye. He wrote, "*Mbuzi* [goat] (his nickname for me), I've got two things for you to consider. Let's take our vacation together in December. I'd like to go to at least two game preserves in Kenya, especially Ngorongoro Crater."

That got my immediate attention! He continued. "Ken, the PCV I worked with in the Ministry of Sport and Culture before I took over here when Mike Davis got hurt, is arranging for a group of ten to twelve to climb Mt. Kilimanjaro. If you join us, you'll be number ten. I hope you'll agree to go. Please let me know *posachedwa* [ASAP]. If yes, I'll send details by return mail."

I answered Bill's letter that afternoon. I was so excited I couldn't stand it.

On my 24th birthday, December 1, 1967, I hitchhiked from Nsiyaludzu to Lilongwe. Bill and I pampered ourselves for one night by staying at the Hotel Lilongwe, one of the poshest in the country. The next afternoon we thumbed to Lusaka, Zambia, most of the way in the back of an open lorry in the rain, over many washboard roads. We arrived around 4:00 a.m. We collapsed from exhaustion in an

121

African hostel, awoke at 11:00 a.m., and then went to have breakfast before taking a cold shower.

Bill and I were together for all but two of the forty days we were away. We hitchhiked to Ndola, where we tried to obtain visas to visit the Congo, but the obligatory wait was too long. Then we hitched from Kapiri Mposhi, Zambia, on the yet-to-be-paved Great North Road, 1,000 miles to Dar es Salaam, Tanzania, in two-and-a-half days. Again, we were beaten to a pulp from riding in the back of a Land Rover.

After exploring Dar with two Peace Corps staff secretaries, we thumbed to Nairobi, which was yet another grueling, challenging trek. At one stop along the way, I surreptitiously photographed two Masai women using expressed breast milk to soften some leather. I had to be extra careful because members of the Masai tribe believe that a camera will capture their soul.

When we finally arrived in Arusha, Tanzania, we met up with Ken and the other seven PCVs. Ken had convinced two Swedish women who were volunteering in Swaziland to join our party, which decreased the cost for everyone. Ascending Kili is a challenging, demanding "walk-up," which usually takes five days—three up, two down. The main gate to the national park near Moshe, Tanzania, East Africa, is at 6,000 ft. It takes three days to walk the twenty-one miles to reach Kibo Hut, which is at 15,500 ft., overnighting at two cabins spaced out in between. The climb doesn't require professional equipment (pitons, carabiners, ropes, pickaxes, oxygen)—it just requires that climbers be fit. The route took us through a bit of rainforest. African hawkers along the way charged three times the norm or more for a warm soda or beer. Those were the days before bottled water.

At the second of the three huts we stayed in on the ascent, one of our guys, Jim, began to suffer from high altitude pulmonary edema (HAPE). His lungs filled up with fluid, making it difficult for him to breathe. The treatment is immediate evacuation to the bottom of the mountain. What was amazing is that a much smaller African carried Jim—*piggyback*—down to home base. By the time Jim was examined by a physician, his lungs were almost clear.

The night before the final stage of the climb, we were fed early at Kibo Hut and encouraged to go to bed shortly thereafter. Awakened at 11:00 p.m., we were given hot tea and some cookies for breakfast. After layering up, we set out up the mountain at midnight. The climb gradually became steeper and steeper—the last 15-20 minutes were very tough, indeed, straight up on paths through a series of rocks and boulders. Particularly frustrating was taking two steps forward and sliding back one on the volcanic scree.

Our group reached Gilman's Point at 4:30 a.m. That meant that we had officially climbed Mt. Kilimanjaro. We rested for ten minutes before trekking the extra thirty minutes to the fabled dome of the mountain, Uhuru Peak (oo-WHO-roo), which means "freedom" in Swahili. Bearing the wind and cold, the eleven of us briefly celebrated our triumph of reaching 19,340 ft., then quickly returned to Gilman's Point. After absorbing the most spectacular sunrise, I took a ten-minute nap in the snow.

The rest of our trip went smoothly. We traveled back through Nairobi, where we were invited to a party by some young white Kenyans we had met on the street.

An old wealthy dowager arrived a bit late. She had on a mink stole and a mink hat and was grasping some hand-held glasses. When she spotted me next to the unlit fireplace—it was ninety degrees in the small mansion—she looked me up and down slowly. I was wearing an African print shirt and was smoking a newly acquired Tanzanian meerschaum pipe (a second, of course).

She squawked, "Oh, good God! It's the bloody Peace Corpse!"

Feeding a little boy *ufa wa mtedza* (maize porridge with peanut flour) during a demonstration with mothers and grandmothers.

HEMATOCHEZIA

"Music is forever; music should grow and mature with you,
following you right on up until you die."

Paul Simon

I had been invited to dinner and to spend the night with an American couple, John and Char Woods, and their two young children. The Woods resided in Zomba, the capital of Malawi at that time, located halfway to Blantyre, some fifty miles from my village.

John was the photographer with the United States Agency for International Development (USAID). It was his idea to film a half dozen of my songs outdoors with the Jazz Giants so that they could be used in outreach efforts by both the Ministry of Health and the Ministry of Agriculture. John was a masterful visionary professional. Malawians, especially the masses in rural areas, relish being entertained. For example, to assure that relevant messages are proffered, a Land Rover from the Ministry of Agriculture would circulate through surrounding villages within walking distance, blaring through an enhanced megaphone, announcing that a film about the wonders of fertilizer would be shown in a central location beginning at sundown. Usually a local whitewashed store would be chosen, with the side of that building used as the screen for the film(s).

The show would begin and end with a film featuring me and the Jazz Giants performing a two-and-a-half-minute version of my hit song, *Feteleza* [Fertilizer], which was considerably longer than

125

the original jingle's length of twenty seconds. The remainder of the presentation would feature extension officials who would be more specific about how to use fertilizer properly, the benefits of using it, and where it could be bought locally.

Similarly, the Ministry of Health would use a myriad of my films featuring our singing and playing my songs about how to become healthier—*Ufa wa Mtedza*, the peanut flour hit; *Chakudya Chosanganiza*, the best foods for your children are a mixture, touting a balanced diet; *Sanbani M'manja Mwanu Pochokera ku Chimbudzi*, imploring people to wash their hands after going to the latrine; and a few others.

John knew that I was scheduled to record *Pikani Madzi Akumwa* [Boil Your Drinking Water] with the Jazz Giants at MBC in Limbe, near Blantyre, the following day. He had made arrangements to film that song with a small group of mothers as they were boiling water in the foreground.

I had hitchhiked to Zomba, taken a taxi for a short ride up the side of the Zomba Plateau to the Woods' home. When I arrived, there was no one present except their houseboy, who welcomed me, fetched me a cold beer, and gave me some snacks to keep the wolf from the door. As I sipped and nibbled while listening to the news on their wireless radio, I began to feel abdominal cramps that slowly, yet steadily, increased in intensity. After about an hour, I began to have diarrhea which also increased in frequency and magnitude. By the time the Woods arrived after 8:00 p.m., I had also developed a fever with shaking chills while being camped out on the toilet. I got little sleep that night. The Woods were delayed by a flat tire. It takes a long time to exchange the flat tire with the spare on a Land Rover.

I kept thinking that I might have been suffering from bilharzia, also known as schistosomiasis, the gut version of a malady which was found sporadically in Lake Malawi. A person with the urinary tract form of this disease would usually present to their doctor because of blood in their urine. Similarly, the liver disorder manifested initially as jaundice. Anyone who swam in Lake Malawi was literally taking a chance of not contracting a variant of this dreaded disease.

The next morning I drank two liters of purified water for breakfast. When John stopped by his office to pick up his equipment, I rushed to the toilet. That's when I first noticed copious "bright red blood per rectum," which I soon learned from our PC physician, Dr. Tom Powers, is the definition of hematochezia. Outwardly, I was calm; inwardly, *terrified*.

When we got back in the vehicle, I told John that I needed to report to the Peace Corps office. I could tell he knew I was not well. As soon as Tom Powers obtained my history and examined me cursorily, he took me straight away to be admitted to Queen Elizabeth Hospital. That afternoon I was seen by Dr. Borgstein, the only surgeon in Malawi, an affable Dutch expatriate who was called upon to perform many procedures beyond his specialty of general surgery.

"Doctor Dutch," as he preferred to be called, immediately performed a rudimentary sigmoidoscopy on me, which included three biopsies. He explained that my colon was markedly inflamed and oozing blood, and that the samples he had taken had to be sent to Salisbury, Rhodesia, for evaluation.

"What do I have, Doc? This seems pretty serious to me."

He replied matter-of-factly, "I don't know yet. It could be something infectious, like salmonella, or perhaps schistosomiasis that you picked up while swimming in Lake Malawi. I doubt if it's malaria. So, we shall see as soon as the results get back from Salisbury, which will take at least a week. In the meantime, I will treat you with a broad-spectrum antibiotic."

Doctors Powers and Borgstein conferred privately. I was discharged under the care of Tom Powers who offered me a convalescent bed in his home. I actually began to feel much better once the fever broke.

The bloody diarrhea subsided rapidly once I was put on a strict diet of clear liquids.

Dr. Powers was concerned about me. He was an inexperienced physician who had only one year of clinical training as an intern beyond medical school. After conferring with the PC Director, arrangements were made for me to be sent to Washington, DC, for further evaluation and treatment.

I was crushed! I was also angry at Tom and at the Peace Corps. I had been in Malawi for fourteen months, and my work was far from done.

Physically, I improved rapidly—no more diarrhea, no further bleeding, no more fever, all with a markedly improved appetite. I was still upset with Tom, yet I could not change his mind about being evacuated to DC.

Because the arrangements for me to be sent to the U.S. took a few days longer than expected, I was able to record "Boil Your Drinking Water" with the Jazz Giants. That was part of the compromise with Tom Powers: recording, yes—filming, no.

I was obviously well enough to travel back to DC alone. I was picked up at the airport by a limo and whisked to the Claridge Hotel which was quite near PC-HQ. Interestingly, as we drove into town, tanks were departing the city. Riots had occurred following the assassination of Bobby Kennedy, so the National Guard had been called in to restore order. That was my first taste of reverse culture shock. Everything seemed to be happening at a frenetic pace compared to my usual routine in Malawi, and no one was walking in the road.

The following day I was seen by the gentlest, kindest, most compassionate physician I had ever encountered. Dr. Yankowich was a first-generation Polish gentleman who had earned kudos locally as "the doctor's doctor." I was immediately put at ease with his engaging, caring demeanor as he took his time explaining everything I was to undergo and exactly why.

Hemoatochezia

The next three days involved a colonoscopy, a lower GI radiological examination, and an upper GI radiological exam by Dr. Yankowich. On day four, I was so relieved when Dr. Y. shared that all three investigations were absolutely clear of disease or other abnormality. I was told to report back in one week.

Since my grandmother lived only forty miles away in Baltimore, I decided to stay with her. My grandmother's given name was Lena May, yet *everyone* called her Mom, including me. Mom was the mother of my father, Jack senior. Although poorly educated, she possessed a certain "country wisdom" that was enviable. This included an uncanny ability to size-up strangers quickly and accurately. Furthermore, Mom could always tell immediately if I fibbed to her.

Mom Allison was also the best cook in my world. She was aghast to see me so thin—I was down to 110 pounds after my illness, yet I had weighed 135 upon graduation from college. She prepared all my favorite foods, from spaghetti with meatballs to ham with pineapple to chicken and dumplin's. We enjoyed steamed blue channel crabs together, and she baked cherry and pecan pies, served with vanilla ice cream. I also couldn't get enough cold milk, something I'd not had since leaving for Puerto Rico a year and a half ago. I was in hog heaven until I eventually foundered. I reached the point where I literally could not eat anymore.

After a total of one month back in America, I was released by Dr. Yankowich with a clean bill of health. He recommended that I be allowed to return to Malawi. However, my request to do so was categorically denied by the Peace Corps.

I was informed that I only had another half-year remaining on my contract, and it would not be cost-effective from the Peace Corps' standpoint for me to be allowed to return to Africa. I kept going up the administrative ladder only to be told the same spiel. Finally, in abject desperation, I firmly, yet politely, demanded to plead my case with the Peace Corps Director, Jack Vaughn. Miraculously, I was granted an audience with him.

"Good afternoon, Mr. Allison. May I call you Earl?"

"Well, sir, since even my mother didn't know that my first name is Earl, I actually prefer to be called Jack." That limp joke seemed to ease the tension for both of us.

"Fine, Jack. Let's dispense with any other formalities. Knowing of your appointment with me, I took the liberty of calling your Peace Corps Director in Malawi. Since he strongly endorsed your returning to Malawi, I am signing authorization for you to do so."

"Thank you, Mr. Vaughn. You don't know how much this means to me! I honestly have lots to accomplish before my tour of duty ends, so I'm most grateful to you and Mr. McKay."

I left for Malawi the following evening.

Making a film for the Ministry of Health, featuring
"Boil Your Drinking Water"

JOHN TEMBO

"Music is the greatest communication in the world. Even if people don't understand the language that you're singing in, they still know good music when they hear it."

Lou Rawls

Self-Help Schemes Help to Build the Country of Malawi [Maselfihelpu Sikimu Amathandiza Malawi] is a song I wrote in Chichewa which was inspired by a speech in English by President Banda I'd heard on the radio. In the middle of the song there's a phrase: "The president always tells us (that)..." followed by the punch line title of this song.

Was this political? Borderline political? I honestly had not given this issue *any* thought whatsoever, for our training staff had encouraged us to gently push the idea of self-help enterprises as a major thrust of enhancing community development. Staff were also adamant that getting involved in politics was strictly forbidden.

In my own village, perfect examples of self-help involvement were the six latrines we constructed, male and female, for our medical dispensary, the primary school and the market. Before this endeavor, the latrine [*chimbudzi*, in Chichewa]—(or simply "chim" as referred to by Peace Corps people) at the dispensary was full, and there was none at either the school or in the market.

So where did people go to relieve themselves? In the bush, of course, in the bush. Awkward, inconvenient and unsanitary, to say the least.

After I had recorded this song at MBC with the Jazz Giants, it got decent airtime. I received a few brief notes from fellow PCVs, thanking me for yet another song that they could use to promote their own local projects. In addition, I sang the song *a cappella* during my cooking demonstrations to expand and embellish my teaching.

I didn't hear any negative commentary about the *Self-Help* song, yet a few weeks after we had recorded and released the song, *Make War on Ignorance, Poverty and Disease* [Khonjetsani Umphawi, Kusadziwa ndi Matenda], something unusual occurred.

Again, the English words to the *Make War* song were those of the *Ngawzi* [Chief of Chiefs] His Excellency the President Doctor Hastings "Kamuzu" [Little Root, a popular nickname that was *never* used alone] Banda, words which he stated frequently in his speeches as essential keys to the ongoing development of Malawi:

"We must combat ignorance by improving and expanding education. We must overcome poverty by modernizing our methods of farming and providing more business opportunities. And we must stamp out disease by building modern hospitals and more rural medical dispensaries. Yes, together we must make war on ignorance, poverty and disease!"

I was shocked when the Peace Corps office sent a car from Blantyre to pick me up, unannounced. This was rare for any PCV and had not occurred to me before. There had been no way to forewarn me, for those were the days before cell phones and laptops. Our village dispensary was devoid of a telephone, and there wasn't any electricity in the entire village. The driver delivered a letter to me.

The brief note from the in-country Peace Corps director informed me that I was being summoned by John Z.U. Tembo, the Minister of Finance who was also President Banda's official Chichewa interpreter: I was to explain to him why I had used certain Chichewa words in the *Make War on Ignorance, Poverty and Disease* song.

I remember swallowing hard. John Tembo had earned the

reputation of being a nasty, murderous bastard, and I was fearfully reluctant to stand before him. He was the president's hatchet man. Apparently when the president wanted someone (or more than one) out of the way, Mr. Tembo arranged for them to die mysteriously in a car crash.

Once I was in Mr. Tembo's waiting room, he made me wait for over an hour. The area was smaller than I had anticipated; this was the first minister's office complex I had visited. I had expected something much larger and expressly opulent. The receptionist told me to have a seat. She was neither engaging nor friendly—a definite departure from the warm, outgoing nature of most Malawians. She was seated behind a desk that seemed much too large for the allotted space. The two chairs for waiting were reminiscent of the 1950's—chrome metal frames with thin cheap fabric cushions. The coffee table was too small for those chairs and only boasted of one outdated promotional leaflet which touted Malawian tourism.

Although the walls were white, the waiting room was still drab and austere. It was not the gray or tan drab of eastern *bloc* communist countries at the time, yet dreary just the same. The two large color photographs hanging side by side were those of President Banda and Minister Tembo. The latter was dour and unsmiling, with a hint of fierceness. John Tembo's picture only augmented my anxiety.

"His Excellency Minister Tembo will see you now, Mr. Allison," his secretary announced dryly, without smiling.

When I entered Mr. Tembo's office, I was not offered a seat.

"What do you want?" he demanded dismissively. He was seated behind a huge, luxuriant desk on a large leather chair that looked more like a throne.

"Thank you so much, indeed, sir. I was told that you wanted to see me concerning the words in my latest song, *Make War on Ignorance, Poverty and Disease*," I answered nervously. My voice trailed off and cracked a little. Admittedly, I was frightened—I didn't know what to expect.

I handed him a copy of the Chichewa words to the song. Mr. Tembo took his time reading those words, sneered at me, then cantankerously challenged the word *khongetsani*. He wanted me to use the word *gonjetsani* instead. Both are the polite imperative, meaning "make war, defeat, vanquish, etc."

"*Gonjetsani* is proper Chichewa," he said haughtily. "You have chosen *khonjetsani*, which is antiquated Chinyanja, if not Chingoni. Don't you work with the Angoni tribe in Ntcheu District?"

"Yes, sir, I do. When I looked up both words in the dictionary, they can be used interchangeably, sir."

I could tell that he was becoming quite angry, and because of his rumored reputation, I tried my best to conceal my rising uneasiness. Then I added a tad forcefully, "Aren't you from Dedza, sir? It's my understanding that the Achewa and the Angoni tribes there speak the very same pure language."

John Tembo looked up and grinned. His next question provided me momentary relief.

"What do you want to do with this song?" he inquired in a disarmingly softer tone.

"Sir, I want to use it as an example—actually as *examples* of community development for my village and for the rest of the country."

With that, he shot up, smiled brightly, and shook my hand with both of his, granted me permission to use the song as I saw fit and told me to keep up the good work. What an incredible, totally unexpected "extrication" from what I had anticipated as the jaws of death!

I also enjoyed government-free intervention with my music for the next eighteen months. That is, until the *president* came down hard on me.

FROM THE RADIO TO THE ROADSHOW

"Music is the movement of sound to reach the soul
for the education of its virtue."

Plato

Two guys walk into a bar. But not together.

Following my harrowing experience with John Tembo, I needed a drink, so I popped into an upscale pub that I'd not visited prior. Although it was only 5:30, the place was already hopping.

A "prim and proper" gent sat down next to me and introduced himself as Chip Wood. I never did learn his given first name. On the surface we contrasted mightily: he looked the part of a CEO—tailored suit, fine linen white shirt with expensive cuff links, tasteful silk tie and spit-shined black leather shoes with a matching black leather belt. His aftershave was subtle and decidedly masculine. His presence seemed to fill the room—tall, charismatic, graceful, charming and urbane. My "outfit" was similar to what I wore everyday: light blue oxford short-sleeved shirt, dusty maroon striped tie, khaki pants and desert boots. I didn't use aftershave in the bush.

Although I couldn't compare with Chip's debonair duds, I was one of the better dressed PCVs in Malawi, mainly because I emulated Mr. Chitowe's daily attire.

Chip shared with me that he was the regional manager for Colgate-Palmolive, covering Malawi, Zimbabwe and Zambia. The major thrust of his job was to make inroads into the clothing detergent market, which was dominated by Surf, so much so that Surf was referred to generically for detergent in Malawi. Chip had been born and reared in Zimbabwe, the former Southern Rhodesia, and he had been educated in private schools in South Africa.

As he related his background, Chip kept staring at me in a peculiar way. Finally, I grinned and asked him if I had a bit of spinach in my teeth. He laughed and added, "You're that famous Peace Corps chap who has become somewhat of a folk hero here in Malawi. Although I do not speak Chichewa, I hear your songs on the radio throughout the day, every day."

I agreed that my songs had become incredibly popular countrywide. He ordered another round of drinks and encouraged me to tell him about my work. After filling him in briefly on my work in the village, I shared that my dream was to tour the country, using my panoply of songs to sing and thereby educate rural Malawians about issues dealing with public health: nutrition, cleanliness, using latrines, vector control, self-help schemes, boiling drinking water, etc. Primarily what I lacked was funding, for I knew that the Ministry of Health couldn't afford my proposed project.

Chip kept the drinks flowing and said that he was hoping that there might be a way for us to collaborate. That's all the encouragement I needed, for I'd been thinking this through, over and over, during the past two months. Chip and I both wanted exposure to promote our wares. Obviously, his were his products, especially Fab detergent, in order to be more competitive with Surf. Mine were my public health messages, delivered musically.

I explained my ideas: "Chip, please realize that I hope to reach primary school students and their teachers during the day by lecturing at four surrounding schools before noon, and then inviting everyone to the local chief's compound before dusk to attend our evening concert."

"So how might Colgate-Palmolive be involved?" he inquired. I was encouraged because his enthusiasm was matching mine.

"I'll give a thirty-minute presentation at those four schools. You could probably care less about vector control, but I'll have fun with the kids speaking in Chichewa and singing with a handheld puppet. Your Malawian field rep can accompany me, be introduced as *Bambo Fabu* [Mr. Fab], and say a few brief words about each night's gathering, stressing that many prizes would be given away," I said hopefully.

Chip was sold on the basic idea. He told me that he wasn't interested in micromanaging my health education program. He was delighted when I explained that there would be a question-and-answer period after each song I would sing and that *Bambo Fabu* would pass out small packets of C-P products for each correct answer, including Fab detergent, Palmolive hand soap and Colgate toothpaste and toothbrushes. The entire show would be public health related, including his prizes. I added that I was sorting through how best to use puppetry in our shows each night.

Bingo! During the next hour we struck a deal on a plan that would take me on a journey that would cover the entire country of Malawi. It only took another fifteen minutes to work out the financial arrangements: I was to receive a vehicle plus petrol and a very small *per diem* for expenses. I ended up losing money on the deal.

The next step was for me to convince the Peace Corps/Malawi Director and the Permanent Secretary of the Malawian Ministry of Health that this project was worth pursuing. Both agreed! Shortly thereafter, my rock-and-roll health roadshow extravaganza was on the road!

Prior to leaving on the tour, I initiated a national "Name the Puppet" contest on MBC, sponsored by Coca-Cola. The winner received three cases of Coke, second place, two cases, and the third, one case. The puppet became known as *Bambo Umoyo*, which means Mister Well Being. The Ministry of Health provided me with a Land Rover, a driver and a new small trailer. In addition to the personal vehicle for me and *Bambo Fabu*, they also provided a colorfully printed canvas backdrop that advertised our conjoint effort between the governmental and private sectors. It didn't take as much convincing as I had anticipated that there should be no territorial boundaries when the health of the people was at stake. Fostering that unique relationship in Malawi at that time was a subtle, quiet, pioneering *coup*.

As I kept thinking through how best to utilize the puppet, Albert Einstein's advice helped provide some answers: "I think ninety-nine times and I find nothing. I stop thinking, swim in silence, and the truth comes to me." However, what occurred not long before our first show commenced was particularly fortuitous. As I was dancing with some kids as dusk approached, while the stage, puppet theater, spotlights and generator were being set up, three seven-year-olds—two girls and a boy—greeted me in English, saying very slowly and ever so preciously, "Hello, Ajacki! How are you?"

I patiently waited for each one to ask me individually before responding to each one personally, and very slowly, "I am fine, thank you, and how are you?", as I shook each one's hand.

The kids were ecstatic, as was I. As I asked each one's name, one of the kids inquired if the puppet would be there tonight—the puppet I had held in class earlier that day. Invariably this was a special scene that was to be repeated every night before each performance thereafter.

A little later, as the crowd grew exponentially, I slipped around behind the puppet theater with a simple request of the man behind the curtains. After the show had begun, *Bambo Umoyo* appeared and called out all three kids by name, welcoming them and their parents to the extraordinary evening of learning, entertainment and fun. He then withdrew behind the curtains briefly. The crowd would explode with glee every time.

During the first round of questioning, suddenly the puppet popped up in the tall puppet theater and proclaimed in a booming, thunderous voice in Chichewa, "That's the stupidest answer I've ever heard!" The crowd was wild with enthusiastic laughter. Once it was quiet again,

Bambo Umoyo employed a softer, more inviting tone, "Madam, please try again. Please think about the song you just heard Jack sing. Now please answer, 'Why should we brush the flies out of our babies' eyes?' I know you can do it!"

The young mother with a baby tied securely on her back was obviously scared. She had never been on a stage before, including under a glaring spotlight; she'd neither seen nor spoken into a microphone before, and she'd never been asked to reply to a rather terrifying puppet before. Her dark brown eyes welling with tears, she hesitantly answered inaudibly, the microphone held too far from her quivering lips. When *Bambo Umoyo* encouraged her to take her time and to speak with the microphone held against her lips, she finally responded, "So that our babies will be healthy without eye disease."

Again, the crowd erupted, yet this time with applause of encouraging approval. She had nailed the answer, received words of congratulation from the puppet, applause from the audience, and a packet of Fab detergent from *Bambo Fabu*. Now it was time for me to sing another song.

The paper-mache puppeteer was Jojo, one of the most memorable people I've ever met. He had multiple duties with our traveling health education show: driver of the Land Rover, which towed my small trailer; handyman in setting up our stage and equipment each night; and most importantly, the voice of *Bambo Umoyo*. And what a voice! A sonorous, reverberating bass, coupled with amazingly expressive eyes and facial expressions which were transmitted to the audience through his ebullient personality night after night, masterfully teaching while entertaining flawlessly.

Jojo was a member of the Asena tribe and he was the polar opposite of that group's ignominious reputation among all the other tribes in Malawi—ignorant, stupid, crass, crude, dirty, poor, lazy—the list of negatives was exhaustive. *Nsanje* is literally translated as *jealousy*, a tongue-in-cheek reflection of the least desirable region in the country. Beyond being the poorest area of Malawi and having fellow Malawians disparage them routinely, the legend of Nsanje included having more mosquitoes than anywhere else in the whole wide world. Jojo stood out when we performed among the Asena people when we were in Nsanje District, for he was hardworking, articulate and successful. At best, his fellow tribesmen were ambivalent toward him, with *jealousy* most likely playing a prominent role in explaining their feelings.

We set out on a rigorous, sleep-deprived five-month tour of Malawi, without cellphones, laptops, email or snail mail. Each morning, after having a scone and a cup of tea, I followed through with teaching for thirty minutes at four schools before noon, using every audio-visual aid possible: blackboards, flannel graphs, handouts, posters, puppets and some of my songs. The kids always went bonkers when I would use the puppet to pretend to brush the flies out of their eyes as I sang. *Bambo Fabu* was well received, too. We made sure to invite the teachers, the students and their parents to attend the concert in the evening at the chief's home.

After scrounging around for lunch, we took an afternoon siesta to rest up for the long night. Two hours before sundown we would set up our stage, which included the canvas backdrop that read, "The Ministry of Health, in conjunction with Colgate-Palmolive, Ltd., proudly presents Jack Allison and his Health Education Show"; a tall puppet theater; an 8-track tape unit with two speakers and two microphones; a petrol-powered generator; and a large box of prizes. I then started loudly playing a myriad of musical selections which included recent rock and roll releases from the U.S. and the UK, African pop music from across the continent and traditional Malawian village tunes. We used the music to help draw a crowd. I especially enjoyed dancing with the children, who were initially a tad apprehensive upon seeing the first white person to visit them, yet who warmed up readily when I played and chatted with them in their own language.

Every evening I was thrilled and humbled that so many people gathered for each performance. At dusk we would crank up the generator, which powered the spotlights for the stage and the puppet theater, and the fun would begin.

The format of this first-of-its-kind traveling health show was based on simplicity and repetition, spiced with playfulness and humor—in other words, with fun, fun and more fun! The local health assistant (HA) was always involved logistically with organizing the lecture series in the schools and the evening shows. After innumerable introductions, including the local chief, the HA would introduce each song, then ask the audience to pay particular attention to the words because they would be asked questions after each song for which prizes would be offered. I would then introduce each song, tell them what it was about, sing it, and then turn the question and answer segment back to the HA, who would select random participants from the audience to come onto the stage to answer the questions over our PA system (powered by the battery of the Land Rover).

The star *and* highlight of each show was definitely our puppet, *Bambo Umoyo*, who would burst through the curtains of the puppet theater to pass light-serious judgment on each answer. With each correct answer the representative from Colgate-Palmolive, *Bambo Fabu*, would present prizes as discussed with Chip Wood. During each show I would sing eight health-related songs, including *Ufa wa Mtedza* to open and close the performances. Following the initial question-and-answer periods after each song, the grand finale of each show included yet another Q&A session, with more and more questions about the health messages of the songs, and more prizes earned for correct answers. We would finish each performance around midnight, totally exhausted.

Needless to say, the road show, including the four daily sessions at local primary schools throughout the country, the two-hour pre-show dancing and playful engagement, and the six-hour shows each night for five months was an incredibly demanding schedule. However, who knew that teaching and learning within this format could be so immensely gratifying, yet with so much pleasure! Our traveling health education road show ended up reaching 60,000 Malawians, primarily in the bush.

What was the force or the causative factor(s) or the magic that brought to fruition my dream of sharing my "music with a message" with so many Malawians? Was it kismet? Could it have been serendipity? I choose synchronicity to help explain my chance meeting with Chip Wood that precipitated such a uniquely satisfying, *joyful* experience.

The words that Rumi penned so many years ago rang true for me then, and even to this day:

let the beauty
of what you love
be what you do

YOUR BLOOD COULD SAVE LIVES!

"I believe 100 percent in the power and importance of music."

James Taylor

Only once while I was in Malawi did I receive a telegram. It arrived at the post office in Balaka and languished in my P.O. box for almost a week until the postmaster sent it to me by a trusted man who lived in my village. It read, "Bambo [Mister] Allison STOP P.S. (Permanent Secretary) Ministry of Health requests your presence STOP Please come at earliest convenience STOP Yours sincerely STOP M. Mkandawire."

What a pleasant surprise! Although I had yet to meet Mphatso Mkandawire in person, his reputation among Peace Corps staff and volunteers was esteemed. His support of both the T.B. Project and our Under-Fives' Clinic Project was unquestioned, even with his strained, limited budget.

I hitchhiked into Blantyre and reported first to the Peace Corps office. I wanted to make sure that the leadership staff were aware of this unusual invitation. After waiting over an hour to meet with our director, Monroe McKay, I found him to be upbeat.

"Jack, have no worries. Mr. Mkandawire is a dear friend of the Peace Corps, so most likely he wants a favor from you. I'm just intrigued that he contacted you directly instead of going through my office. We shall see, eh?"

"Monroe, I'm surprised, too, for I've never met the chap. How shall we proceed?"

Monroe asked his secretary to call P.S. Mkandawire's office. We learned that the P.S. was presently in Zomba, testifying before parliament about a pressing issue. She arranged for me to meet with him at 10:00 the following morning.

Monroe graciously invited me to stay at his home. Typically, volunteers stayed at the local African rest house, although that was always fraught with challenges. Peace Corps had procured sleeping bags which had originally been issued for arctic climes. In Malawi, they were extremely hot, to say the least. Although designated for PCV use only, they were used frequently by Malawian men.

Over time these bags became infested with bed bugs. The first time I had stayed at this rest house a young Malawian was awakened and forced to relinquish the PC bag to me. The bed bugs feasted on me all night.

During breakfast the next morning, Monroe and I sipped our coffee, speculating about why I had been summoned to the P.S.' office. In the end we weren't even close.

At 9:45, when I arrived at Mr. Mkandawire's small spartan office, I was ushered in to see him before I could sit down in the tiny waiting area. "Aphiri, it is indeed so very nice to finally meet the most famous Peace Corps Volunteer ever to serve here in Malawi," Mr. M. gushed as he shook my hand vigorously.

"Thank you, sir. But how do you know my clan name?"

"Not many Europeans are offered the honor of having an African clan name bestowed upon them. Because of the popularity of your music, Aphiri, word has gotten around that you have been accepted into our culture so much more than any other volunteer. Please be seated, sir."

Mr. Mkandawire was a rather large man for a Malawian. He looked to be forty years of age and in excellent shape. His round tortoise-shell eyeglasses made him look professorial, and he spoke with a loud stentorian voice. He was an easy guy to like.

Without asking me, Mr. Mkandawire ordered tea and biscuits (cookies to the British). We shared small talk for another five minutes or so when he suggested that I call him by his nickname, "Gift."

"Aphiri, by now you know the translation of *mphatso*. It means gift, and that's what my wife and close friends call me."

"I am honored to do so, sir. From now on, Gift it shall be."

I was amazed at how relaxed and unhurried he was, even by Malawian standards. It wasn't until we began to enjoy our second cup of tea that he got around to talking about the issue at hand. "Aphiri, Dr. Dutch for years has been pleading with the Ministry of Health that he is in perpetual need of blood transfusions on a daily basis. Not all Europeans fancy giving blood, and most Malawians won't give blood for a host of reasons." Gift went on to explain that Europeans would give blood readily for a family member or friend in need.

Malawians, on the other hand, held many superstitions about blood. He emphasized that what was called for was a focused education campaign directed at both groups. He also mentioned that he was particularly encouraged by the popularity of my bilingual jingle for Mobil petrol.

"That's where you come in, Aphiri. I have garnered permission from the Minister of Health to ask you to please write and record a bilingual song, in English and Chichewa, about blood donation. Once you've done that, the ministry will create an educational program which will emphasize key points from the lyrics. What do you say, Aphiri? I obviously hope that you will say *yes!*"

I paused—not because I was in doubt of what I was about to agree to. I realized that the answer to the question Monroe and I had mused earlier was that I was being treated as a peer—as a staff member of the Peace Corps rather than a mundane volunteer.

That was a powerful moment. I couldn't hold back my enthusiasm! This was the kind of project I fantasized about. I agreed on the spot to compose the song quickly, rehearse it with the Jazz Giants, and arrange to have it recorded at MBC. The turnaround time was less than two weeks, for Mr. M. helped to cause things to fall into place so much more quickly than what even Malawians referred to as "African time."

The song was played quite frequently on the radio because MBC was controlled by the government. The European community—mostly British, yet included Americans, Portuguese, Germans, Swedes, Italians, French and Greeks—responded beyond what had been projected. Blood began to be stockpiled at both Queen Elizabeth Hospital in Blantyre and Lilongwe General Hospital, totally unique to both facilities.

Things were sorely different with Malawians—very few showed up to donate blood. In addition to their superstitions about blood, I was told that they feared the very sight of it. In Malawi there is a longstanding belief in vampires, particularly involving Westerners, who especially during times of famine, work with the government to collect blood in exchange for food.

Many Malawians believe in blood-drinking monsters. This belief is said to go back over 3,500 years to the time of the Babylonians. Furthermore, something strange began to recur in the ghettoes around Blantyre and Limbe—a series of murders in which the victims' throats were slashed deeply enough to involve both carotid arteries, causing them to exsanguinate in a horrific pool of their blood.

Fear became rampant in both communities, compounded by an increase in the number of murders, and a dearth of clues and leads for the police authorities. Each person who was interviewed said that "they hadn't heard any evil, didn't see any evil, and didn't know any evil."

When my song was pulled from the radio, the murders ceased abruptly. Gift penned me a long apologetic letter, stating that our noble visionary work was surely not in vain. He hoped that someday soon our blood donation campaign would begin afresh, anticipating better results from his brother and sister Malawians. I was ambivalent—hopeful, yet doubtful.

The murders were never solved.

THIRD-YEAR EXTENSION

"If music be the food of love, play on."

William Shakespeare

Toward the end of my two-year tour with the Peace Corps I applied to extend for a third year. My national health education/music tour had not been completed and I had other public health projects that also warranted attention. In late November 1968, I had been summoned to the PC office in Blantyre two days before the rest of our public health team of volunteers. They were going to be completing the necessary paperwork, physical exams and other terminal issues known as close of service (COS). It was the end of their two years in Malawi. I was pleased and a bit surprised to see Gail there.

"It's so good to see you, *Anachisale* [Gail's clan name]. What are you doing in Blantyre so early?" I asked as I leaned in closer, hoping down deep that she wanted to extend, too. Gail and I had dated a few times during our training sessions in both California and Puerto Rico as well as a few more infrequent times in-country. I would have relished seeing her more often—it's just that we lived two hundred miles apart, which was really quite far in Malawi.

"Hopefully the same as you. I honestly don't know if my request for an extension came through, but I'm encouraged to have been invited to report early to Blantyre," she responded with an inviting smile. "It's good to see you here, too!"

PC Director Monroe McKay greeted us with a big smile and asked how our travels into Blantyre had gone. Both of us had hitchhiked into town. Gail's trip from Rumphi up north had taken one-and-a-half days; mine, five-and-a-half hours.

Monroe got right to the point. "I have a proposition for both of you. A host of others in your group has applied to extend for an additional year with the Peace Corps. It has been decided that *if and only if* you both agree to our proposal, the two of you will be offered this opportunity to extend. We are not offering this to any of the other applicants." Monroe was a salesman *par excellence*. He went on to explain the two facets of this unique situation.

Peace Corps had been evolving toward more in-country training over the past two years. Language and culture would now be taught in-house. Since Gail had scored the highest in Chitumbuka and I in Chichewa on the Foreign Service Institute test at pre-COS, Monroe was offering us the chance to become language coordinators for each incoming group of PC trainees.

After the latter had completed their training, been sworn in, and sent to their assigned town or village to begin work, Gail and I would be allowed to continue with our usual daily routine until the next group of PC trainees arrived in-country.

Then Monroe added a seal-the-deal bonus perk. "After your paid month of leave at home, or wherever you decide to spend your vacation time, we will arrange an additional three weeks of language teacher training, geared toward your new assignment here. These educational activities will be split between Peace Corps language experts at headquarters in DC and at the Chilton Language Learning Center in Philadelphia. What do you think?" He smiled and leaned back in his chair.

We both signed on immediately! What we later learned once our new job had commenced was that there was yet another very positive perquisite we had not anticipated. We were to be treated as junior PC staff members, which meant that during language training stints we were to be afforded the *ultimate* perk—use of a PC vehicle.

During lunch together to celebrate our extension, Gail was eager to share some beguiling ideas. "Since I didn't know you were going to be extending as well, I had started thinking about what my options—now *our* options—might be for traveling home. We'll have prepaid airline tickets back to the States. Why don't we investigate whether we can visit Nigeria where we had trained for initially? If you're free after lunch, let's stop by the travel agency."

"I'm glad I thought of that," I teased. I was not aware that amending my ticket was a possibility. As we started adding other possible stops in West Africa, which Gail jotted down, we both became more and more excited.

The travel agent was a thirty-year-old British woman named Beatrice who was affable and quite experienced. After sharing our notes with her, she efficiently mocked up an inviting itinerary in less than twenty minutes.

She reported enthusiastically, "I have great news for both of you! You can fly to Nairobi, Kenya, where you'll change planes for Lagos, Nigeria; Accra, Ghana; Abidjan, Ivory Coast; Monrovia, Liberia; and Dakar, Senegal, then on to your chosen airports in the U.S., *at no additional charge*! Please note that I strongly recommend that you forego Freetown, Sierra Leone. Following a recent *coup*, there is dangerous civil unrest there."

We were ecstatic! Beatrice suggested that we get back with her the next day about how long we wanted to stay in each country.

Unfortunately, our trip had to be postponed. As we were leaving the travel agency, Gail stepped off the curb into an unseen hole in the pavement and fell awkwardly. She felt immediate intense pain in her left knee. Beatrice had witnessed this as she was standing in the doorway to see us off. She offered to help in any way she could, which she did a few days later. I helped Gail limp slowly back to the African guest house where we both were staying. That night, when I went to her room to check on her before dinner, I noticed that her knee had swollen considerably. She told me that she had difficulty bending it and walking on it.

The next morning, I walked quickly over to the Peace Corps office and asked that Gail be brought in by vehicle since she could barely stand up. The PC physician examined her and referred her immediately to Dr. Dutch, a general surgeon—there was not one orthopaedic surgeon in Malawi. That afternoon she was operated on successfully for repair of a torn medial meniscus.

The next afternoon I visited Gail in the hospital to wish her well in her recovery. I was concerned about her. I also had no idea how long it would be before she'd be able to leave Malawi.

Gail was in excellent spirits when I arrived. After she had filled me in on the last afternoon and evening, she said unexpectedly, "If you'll wait until I've been discharged, including rehab, I'd like to travel home with you as we had planned with Beatrice." Then she added with an enticing smile, "This morning she hand-delivered a proposed itinerary with suggested dates for each stopover for our consideration. She had not expected me to be up in a chair at 10:00 a.m. Would you like to take a peek?"

"Hmmm. Please show me what she brought."

I was impressed at how well Gail was doing after surgery, and I was totally amazed that Beatrice had followed through in such an unconventional way. She had done a marvelous job in anticipating our needs, for she had picked up readily that we wanted to spend more time in Nigeria. I returned the next morning to plot out our proposed trip in more detail.

Gail was doing far better than I had anticipated. Although she was not yet allowed to do any weight bearing, she was ambling with ease down the hall on her new set of crutches. We then mapped out an ambitious trip, beginning with Nigeria.

Third-Year Extension

While Gail was rehabbing with daily physical therapy sessions, I arranged to continue my national musical public health tour for the next two weeks, Monday through Friday. She and I began seeing more of each other "outside of work" on those abbreviated weekends. After our extension for that additional year with the Peace Corps, our relationship got serious.

VACATION IN WEST AFRICA

"Music is the language of the spirit. It opens
the secret of life bringing peace, abolishing strife."

Kahlil Gibran

G ail healed rapidly. Sixteen days post-op she was ready to begin our vacation. The next two weeks were magical for us. Our trip was a montage thoroughly reflective of young love—intimate, exciting, carefree, eager, naïve, fun, idealistic, exploring—replete with open communication and the sharing of each other's hopes and dreams, with feelings ranging from hopeful exuberance to cautious vulnerability. We discovered that we really liked spending time together.

Upon landing in Lagos, Nigeria, Gail and I agreed that West Africans were noticeably different from Malawians—less polite, more pushy, less patient, more demanding, less friendly, and definitely louder. These perceived attributes were especially magnified in Nigeria in comparison with Ghana, Ivory Coast, Liberia and Senegal.

During our two days in Lagos we tried in vain to get tickets to see Pele and his Santos soccer club. They were there on an international tour for a series of exhibition matches to display the extraordinary skills of the King of Soccer. Legend has it that two years earlier both factions in the Nigerian Civil War had agreed to a cease-fire for forty-eight hours so they could watch Pele play an exhibition game in Lagos.

Travel in Africa has always been challenging and is even more so when financial resources are limited. After hitchhiking the seventy-five miles to Ibadan to visit with some dear former PC training staff members, we hitched another four hundred and fifty miles to the city of Kano in the north. The roads outside of the cities and towns were similar to those in Malawi, full of potholes and pervasively dusty, and knowing that we also had to hitchhike all the way back to Lagos was disheartening but necessary on our limited budget.

Kano was a city also very different from any we had experienced in Africa, especially Old Town. It is truly ancient, with a vibrant history of trade, architecture and Islamic culture. Kurmi Market, founded in 1463, teemed with activity, accompanied by the sounds and smells associated with so many people busily plying their eclectic wares. The market was *enormous*, with so many small winding paths that we had to be extra careful not to get lost in such a large, unwieldy maze. I'd never seen so many small shops. Everything seemed to be for sale—garden vegetables, yams, maize, cassava, sorghum, millet, rice, and spices galore, as well as textile materials, leather goods, gold and silver jewelry, baskets of all shapes, sizes and colors, knives, swords, and even cattle and chickens on the periphery.

As trainees we had been apprised of the "dash system," a culturally accepted form of bribery. Returned PCV staff had related that in order to retrieve a package from home at the post office, they were expected to dash—to give the postal clerk a small cash "gift" to receive the parcel.

While at the market I approached a Nigerian who was lounging comfortably in the shade, regaled in a beautifully embroidered white flowing robe with a matching kufi cap, and I held out my hand and said, "Dash me!" Without missing a beat, he filled up my hand with coins. He had spontaneously called my bluff, and I was dumbfounded. I immediately returned the coins, thanked him profusely and scurried away. Both the gentleman and Gail laughed at length at my silly, awkward display.

Another cultural highlight was watching Tuaregs, semi-nomadic Berbers, come riding into town on mighty steeds from the desert to the north, dressed in long, flowing black robes and black tagelmust headgear, brandishing long fearsome doubled-edged swords. They looked *fierce*.

GAIL AND I HAD RECALLED TWO agriculture-rural development (Ag-RD) PCVs with whom we had overlapped in La Jolla. We inquired about their whereabouts at the City Planning Office.

Gail asked the receptionist, "Do you happen to know where we might find Ted Thompson and Chad Collingsworth, two of our dear friends from Peace Corps training?"

The young woman surprised us by saying, "Yes, their shared office is on the second floor."

Ted and Chad were as astonished to see us as we were to reconnect with them. It had been almost two-and-a-half years since we'd seen them off for Nigeria.

"Hey, what's the deal? Both of your names are on the door as Co-Directors of City Planning? Good grief! You guys are living in tall cotton!" I exclaimed.

Since it was almost closing time, Ted and Chad took us to their lovely, modern, tastefully decorated apartment. Their story was long, involved and spellbindingly fascinating. The short version was that they had consummated so many successful planning projects for Kano that the City Council had promoted them far beyond their expectations. And because the Peace Corps was paying their salaries, the government officials were beyond pleased with the arrangements. Ted and Chad, too, had extended with the Peace Corps for at least another year.

After enjoying a delicious meal of lamb in a spicy peanut sauce, rice, foo-foo (the West African version of *nsima*), vegetable salad and fabled Star beer, we finally got to taste palm wine for the first time, a legendary libation we'd heard so much about during training. We also got to dance to high-life music before turning in. Ted and Chad were marvelous hosts, and Gail and I were impressed with their outstanding accomplishments as PCVs.

NEITHER OF US WAS PARTICULARLY EXCITED about our visit to Accra, Ghana, although we were disappointed that we didn't have time to visit Kumasi, the capital of the Ashanti Region. The Ashanti tribe has a rich cultural heritage of being fierce warriors. They have a special handshake—they hold out their left hand because the left hand holds the shield, whereas the right hand holds the spear. Trust is demonstrated by putting down your shield, thereby freeing up your left hand.

Our itinerary was changed because of severe winter weather in the States, so we stopped next in Abidjan, Ivory Coast, which was a fascinating place. The airline not only paid for our hotel room, they also provided a free lunch and dinner at the most expensive restaurant in town which overlooked the city and the ocean. After "overdosing" on fresh lobster at noon, we had difficulty finishing our supper of steak *au poivre* and coffee ice cream *parfaits*.

Our visit to Monrovia, Liberia, began with a jolt—the taxi driver wanted $2.00 per mile for the 37-mile trek from Roberts Field Airport into the city. I managed to talk him down to $52.00, including tip. Liberia was the second African nation to welcome African Americans, especially freed slaves, a safe haven. Sierra Leone was the first nation to make such an offer. While we were there, a recent group of African Americans had decided to move "back to their roots." Naively, they failed to take into consideration the massive cultural differences between Liberians and Americans. Their efforts to live in the bush with their proclaimed "soul brothers and sisters" did not last long. Most returned home to the States. A few moved into Monrovia where they established eateries such as hamburger joints and soul food restaurants. The ones we met were disenchanted and rather disillusioned.

During those two weeks in West Africa, Gail and I were able to complete the itinerary that Beatrice had fashioned for us, inclusive of Goree Island, located off the coast of Dakar, the bustling, sprawling capital of Senegal. Goree Island was the symbol of slave trade from the 15th-19th century. Its architecture was a stark contrast between the ghastly slave quarters and the stately homes of the slave traders.

Needless to say, those two weeks together were *enchanting*!

Achitowe (left) was the best man in my wedding.

TRANSITIONS

My second taste of reverse culture shock was when I returned to the States from our vacation in West Africa. There was so much hustle-bustle at a high rate of speed compared to the slow easy pace of village life. Having not watched television for over two years, most of the programs seemed vapid, even dumbed down.

It was so good to reconnect with my mother, stepfather and my five brothers. Mom's cooking was so delicious, and she spoiled me by preparing my favorites, especially homemade spaghetti. However, when a discussion of presidential politics came up over dinner my second night home, my stepfather and I had a major falling out. I was angered when he proudly announced that in the primary he had voted for George Wallace, the blatantly racist four-time governor of Alabama. Then he repeated something he had asked *before* I'd left for PC training two years prior:

"Why do you want to go over there to work with niggers when we have plenty of niggers here?"

I said nothing. I excused myself from the table, packed my bag, and hopped a bus for Chapel Hill early the next morning.

Gail and I eventually met up in Washington, D.C., where we received excellent training as language coordinators. That included an extra week at the Chilton Language Institute in Philadelphia before spending yet another week of language instruction at Peace Corps headquarters in D.C.

Because the Peace Corps was providing our airline tickets back to Malawi, Gail cleverly arranged for us to return via Rio de Janeiro, Brazil; Johannesburg, Durban and Witwatersrand, South Africa; Victoria Falls, Zambia; and Harare, Zimbabwe. The additional cost per ticket was only $30.00! Again, what a fantastic trip!

Rio was romantic, perhaps the most romantic city I've ever visited. Gail and I were able to find a small, clean, quiet hotel near Ipanema Beach. Brazil had recently undergone a series of monetary devaluations, so when I gave the desk clerk a large escudo bill, asking him to break it up for me for tip money, he replied, "Sir, this bill is worth less than twenty cents in American money."

Embarrassed, I requested a brief tutorial about Brazilian money. The clerk willingly obliged.

Ipanema was a pristine beach with many bikinied young women and an equal number of buff young men. During the three days we were in Rio we didn't see one pregnant woman in public.

Visiting the enormous statue *Corcovado* [Christ the Redeemer] was a treat as was having a light supper with a succulent bottle of Portuguese wine atop Sugarloaf Mountain. The cable car ride to-and-fro was a panoramic delight.

Johannesburg was a modern bustling city. Gail and I joined the disco scene one night. The young people were friendly. *They* were white. *We* were white.

A very unpleasant occurrence happened in Jo'burg. Gail and I had left our watches back at the youth hostel where we were staying. When I asked an African for the time, I felt a very strong blow to my upper left arm. I wheeled immediately. I was staring into the angry eyes of a policeman. It was obviously he who had belted me with his baton.

"Why in hell did you hit me?" I said.

"Careful, my boy, with how you speak to a police officer. One more comment like that, I will have you hauled away to jail," was his stern reply.

"So may I ask again why you hit me so hard?"

"Because you were fraternizing with an indigenous Bantu. That is strictly disallowed. Next time ask a white person," was his answer.

The next morning, I had a huge bruise where I'd been struck.

Gail and I hitchhiked to Durban and back to Jo'burg. Durban is South Africa's equivalent to Miami Beach. We noticed that park benches and areas on the beach were relegated among "Only" signs for Whites, Coloureds (mixed race), Asians (Indians and Chinese), and Bantu. Those for whites were in the vast majority, with very few for Bantu.

Witwatersrand was an ultra-conservative town politically. Without being prompted, every white South African we encountered there was an openly avid apologist for apartheid. Gail and I were eager to get back to Jo'burg.

Victoria Falls was thunderous and quite misty. The rainy weather kept us from fully enjoying the views. A troupe of baboons in the parking lot brought back a memory of an earlier close encounter I'd experienced with baboons while transporting my dog, Iwe, from Blantyre to Nsiyaludzu Village on my motorcycle.

By the time we had returned to Malawi it was already March 1969, near the beginning of our language coordination involvement with the first of three PC training groups. We also decided to do a few things:

We applied to graduate school and we took the Graduate Record Examination in Blantyre after taking time to study the prep manual. Both of us did well on the GRE.

The other decision was to get married. First, we were married by the District Commissioner in Rumphi, which was required by law in Malawi. Then we were in a day-long traditional African ceremony in Bolero, Gail's nearby village. That celebration was replete with many

Gail and me, before our civil wedding ceremony in Rumphi.

long speeches; African gifts including an elephant's tail, wooden bowls, carvings, ivory rings and bracelets; and cloth for making dresses and shirts. There was also plenty of roasted beef, village beer, music and dancing. That celebration lasted all night.

My small bachelor's party the night before was held in a local bar. When the waitress tried to converse in Chitumbuka, the language of the North, with Achitowe, who was my best man, he mumbled in English, "I don't understand a word she's saying, Aphiri."

My retort was, "Welcome to my world!"

Gail and I honeymooned on the Nyika Plateau. There was frost on the ground every morning so snuggling under extra blankets each night was necessary to stay warm. A British park ranger let us borrow his shortwave radio, so I stayed up all night listening to Neil Armstrong's venture, the first man to walk on the moon.

A few months later Gail and I actually got to see video of that historic event at the USAID office in Blantyre. Many Malawians who crowded into that small space refused to believe that what they were watching was true.

Village procession for our wedding in Bolero Village.

America's Heroes

jack allison

DRAFTED!

*"After silence, that which comes closest to expressing
the inexpressible is music."*

Aldous Huxley

After arriving at Camp Leghorn, a mammoth nondescript sprawl populated with hordes of servicemen dressed in olive drab and camouflage, I stood out, being the only one mufti clad. When I sat down before an eighteen-year-old private who began filling out the physical exam forms before examining me, I noticed that he had filled in "blood pressure 120/80, pulse 72."

"Sir, aren't you going to take my blood pressure and pulse and verify other portions of my physical? For Pete's sake, I've flown all the way from Africa *for this crap?*" I asked with an edge.

"Okay. First of all, sir, don't call me sir. I'm not an officer. So, you want me to take your blood pressure and pulse, I'll do just that," he said sarcastically with a Brooklyn accent. After pumping up the BP cuff to a most uncomfortable level and going through the motions of taking my pulse and other cursory parts of the exam, he didn't change his original numbers. I honestly wanted to slap him.

The written part of the exam was a bad joke, as well. The issues were banal, and the questions were at a fifth-grade level. In less than one hour, including a "visit" with a physician who never examined me, I was summarily informed in less than thirty seconds that I was fit to return to Africa. What a monumental waste of taxpayer resources and my valued time. This entire situation was foreboding.

WHEN A RASH UNDER ONE OF my arms was slowly getting worse, I asked to be evaluated by the Peace Corps physician at the PC office in Blantyre. After that healing consultation, Associate Director Andy Oerke asked to see me in his office.

"I have a registered letter for you which arrived yesterday. Looks like it's from your draft board," he said.

I quickly opened the letter to discover that I was required to report for a pre-draft physical exam—in *Italy*, of all places! This occurred just one month after Gail and I had returned from our vacation in West Africa and the States. The letter was ominous, catching me off-guard and concerning me greatly. The envelope even contained the sheets to be completed for the physical, along with a passel of tickets and a generous *per diem* check. When I showed the government letter and forms to our PC physician, Roger Hofmeister, he and I were at a loss.

"These forms are the same for the military, public health service, Peace Corps or any other governmental agency. I'll bet you a nickel to a doughnut that your draft board doesn't trust Peace Corps docs to be honest about your physical examination. That's why you're being required to report to Camp Leghorn in Italy," he related, concern in his voice.

This situation was even more stressful since Gail and I were quite busy with our respective jobs, planning a July wedding together, studying for the GRE, applying to graduate schools, and beginning to plan our trip home in late December, when our three-year tour would be up.

GAIL AND I WORKED HARD WITH both the language instructors and the PCVs on the language programs for which we had been allowed to extend for a third year. We especially enjoyed and appreciated our added interchanges with the volunteers each evening. She and I were so gratified and proud of all three groups of incoming PCVs when they scored the best ever on the FSI language test immediately following training before their reporting for duty as secondary school teachers. A few even continued to write letters to us in Chitumbuka or Chichewa after we had returned to the USA.

Peace Corps staff were also quite pleased, yet Gail and I were pleasantly surprised when our request was granted for us to visit with each volunteer to check on their progress with language acquisition. The PC office even allowed us an allowance to buy small gifts for the volunteers, knowing that we would be staying at each site in sleeping bags on the floor.

Then disaster struck! We were on our way back to Blantyre after covering most of the country. During one of these evaluation visits, I was summoned to a principal's office to receive an urgent call. It was from Associate Director Oerke at PC-HQ who was rambling on excitedly.

"Jack, I hope that you're sitting down, for we've just received a telegram stating that you've been drafted into the U.S. Army. You're to report for induction in Sebring, Florida, one month to the day after you're scheduled to leave Malawi. I know this is a shock! Finish up what you and Gail are doing, then come on into the office to discuss logistics. Sorry. You're the only volunteer to have ever been drafted while serving in Malawi."

I was *stunned*—it was thirteen days before my 26th birthday, December 1st. Back then when one reached 26 years of age, one was no longer eligible for the draft. And as a *non sequitur*, the first ever lottery for the draft was held that day. My number was 156, which was considered uncomfortably close to being called up.

I had been in Malawi for less than a year when I was introduced to Sam Hobgood, an American who worked as a USAID staff member in Zomba. We had been invited to attend a rare event for me, a cocktail party put on by one of his compatriots. As Sam and I chatted about each other's projects, he happened to mention that he was an avid ham radio enthusiast and that he'd received an unusual call.

"Just the other night I received a call from an Ambrose Sturgess in Florida who asked an unusual number of questions about you personally. I told him how suddenly you had become quite famous here in Malawi because of your music."

I decided to change the subject, not wanting to comment for fear that anything I might say would be relayed back to Sturgess. I only bumped into Sam twice more during the remainder of my PC tour, yet both times he made a point of reminding me that Sturgess had been calling him periodically, specifically to get an update about me. Being targeted by Sturgess was enormously disconcerting to me.

When I extended for the third year with the Peace Corps, I decided not to ask Sturgess a question to which I already knew the answer.

Looking back, the history with my draft board—especially with its chair, Ambrose Sturgess—is telling. I turned eighteen on December 1, 1961, while a freshman at Warren Wilson College. I had been reminded by the dean's office that I was required to register for the draft in Asheville, which I did, and those forms were forwarded to my own draft board in Sebring, Florida.

Because the war was heating up in Vietnam, some of these agencies required permission to leave the U.S.A., no matter the circumstance. My board definitely did. When I called Mr. Sturgess to request permission to go to Europe for five weeks with the UNC Men's Glee Club, he was reluctant to provide that approval.

Drafted!

"You're almost finished with five years of college, Mr. Allison. You'll soon be considered for the draft—that is, unless you'd rather enlist in the service," he said rather sternly. I remained silent, as did he for an uneasy period. Finally, he added, "I reckon you can go."

I hesitated before reminding him that I'd been accepted to serve with the Peace Corps for two years in Ghana, West Africa, when he went on a mini-rant which included such phrases as "draft dodging," "a waste of taxpayers' dollars," and "why would someone want to do that?" I patiently waited for him to wind down before thanking him for allowing me to go to Europe, then politely asked him if the board would please release me to report for duty with the Peace Corps. After a few more editorial mutterings, he said yes to my request, although the reluctance in his voice was evident.

Gail and I shared this horrific emotional crusher in abject disbelief. She and I had planned an elaborate journey back to the States. We had bought a 1948 Morris Minor and had had the engine rebuilt, and we had rearranged our airline tickets home to travel east instead of west by simply topping-up the fee for the tickets that were provided by the U.S. government. The additional charges were quite reasonable.

Our grand scheme was to drive to Botswana to visit with a former PC Associate Director and his family; drive down to Cape Town, South Africa, to take in Table Mountain, Robben Island (where Nelson Mandela was imprisoned for so many years) and the wineries of Stellenbosch; drive up the Garden Route to Durban, South Africa's answer to Miami; then sail second class passage, with the car, to Bombay via the Seychelle Islands, and eventually to Calcutta, after stopping for a few days in Nepal. We were then going to abandon the car—it was against the law to sell it—and fly to Los Angeles, with scheduled stops in Rangoon, Saigon, Manila, and Honolulu.

And that's not all! We had planned on picking up a new pre-paid Toyota Corolla in Torrance, California, drive to Denver as a newly married couple to meet Gail's parents, drive to Florida to meet mine, and then drive to Philadelphia, where we had hoped to take an immersion course in French—all of this before graduate school classes were to begin in August 1970 at the School of Public Health at the University of North Carolina in Chapel Hill.

Needless to say, being drafted completely dashed those elaborate ambitious plans.

PERSONA NON GRATA

"No matter how corrupt, greedy, and heartless our government, our corporations, our media, and our religious & charitable institutions may become, the music will still be wonderful."

Kurt Vonnegut

The songs and jingles that I had written and recorded in Malawi were quite popular with Malawians. Every day, my songs were played frequently on the only radio station in the country, MBC. *Time* magazine had done an article about my health education songs and jingles which was reprinted in *Reader's Digest*. Soon thereafter, *Newsweek* published a similar piece.

The problem began with the publication of a second *Newsweek* article that both praised my music *and* proclaimed that I was more popular with the Malawian people than their own president, Dr. Hastings "Kamuzu" Banda.

Dr. Hastings Banda
photo c/o Wikimedia Commons,
National Archives of Malawi

President Banda was beside himself with anger. In early December 1969, he made a series of speeches over a three-day period to the Malawi Congress Party (MCP), which was the only political party allowed in Malawi.

Day One

"Azibambo ndi Azimai [Gentlemen and Ladies]," he began sternly. "As we continue our plenary session of MCP, there is something important I need to share with you." As I listened to his speech after work with three fellow PCVs over a few early evening beers, I was braced for something serious—the president always introduced bad news on the airwaves with those same words—"… there is something I need to share…."

The *Ngwazi,* President Banda's lauded nickname, translated as "chief of chiefs, expert, skilled, brilliant" in Chichewa, lapsed into an accelerated, harsh diatribe, "Too many members of the Peace Corps are unkempt and slovenly. Men sport unruly beards and don't dress in accord with our cultural standards. The wearing of shorts and tee shirts is unacceptable!"

The president continued with even more vigor. "Peace Corps women are fond of wearing so-called mini-skirts, even though our national policy forbids that blasphemous attire!"

Banda never gave a speech in his native tongue. Perhaps having been away from Malawi for over thirty years without speaking Chichewa was the reason. Occasionally, he would correct his interpreter, for his speeches were translated as he spoke. But because he did so in such a conspicuous manner, word on the street and quietly in pubs was that he could no longer speak Chichewa properly.

That night we PCVs groused about the president's tenor, tone and pinpoint focus on the Peace Corps. Ned, a PCV teacher from Liwonde who was in Blantyre for a teachers' training conference, asked, "What's the old goat up to? He frequently goes after the Peace Corps, but this evening he sounds *really* ticked off."

Our mutual concern was heightened the next evening when the president continued his harangue. Moreover, it got personal for me early into his speech.

Day Two

Banda began by criticizing me and especially my music, stating that it was a corrupting influence on Malawian youth. I had anticipated what was coming next, for Banda's voice cracked slightly. "Jack Allison sings songs in Chichewa, yet he makes so many atrocious errors! And his pronunciation of our native language is deplorable!" he exclaimed.

His rant went on for over an hour, decrying the manifold egregious violations that PCVs committed repeatedly. He claimed that far too many secondary school lessons being taught did not conform with the government syllabus, from which all teachers had to expound. Then, he ended his speech by banning my music.

"That contemptible son-of-a-bitch!" groused Derek, an agriculture PCV from Mikolongwe, just east of Blantyre. "He's threatened by you, Jack, for he doesn't want that *Newsweek* article to get circulated widely. Perhaps his iron-fisted rule might get challenged from within."

"Hey, you guys, I was afraid he'd be angry about the article, but *I* didn't write it."

Judy, a TB volunteer, who had come into town from Chikwawa to see her boyfriend Derek, wondered if things might get worse before the MCP convention was concluded. We were worried that she might be right.

Day Three

The four of us had decided to get together again for the last evening of the Malawi Congress Party assembly to listen to the president's closing speech. President Banda launched right in, continuing to criticize the Peace Corps at large. He blasted my music again, which he had already banned.

Then he culminated that part of his tirade: "I've had enough!" Banda declared forcefully. "I hereby proclaim Jack Allison *persona non grata*. He is no longer welcome in this country. Allison must leave Malawi with dispatch!"

I was rocked to my core. After the publication of the last *Newsweek* article, I knew it was inevitable that President Banda would react negatively. However, to be dismissed so callously, and on national radio, was to me, petulant, cruel and deeply hurtful.

Although I was already scheduled within less than two weeks to leave Malawi at the end of my three-year tour of duty, I wasn't prepared logistically or emotionally to be tossed out so abruptly.

Ironically, I never wore shorts, tee shirts or sandals during the three years I was in Malawi, and I never sported a beard or long hair. Rather, I wore a tie to work every day, as did my Malawian counterpart, even though we lived deep within the bush.

Ned, Judy and Derek gathered around me and patted me on the shoulder, assuring me that I was not to blame for getting kicked out of Malawi.

However, Banda wasn't finished. He delivered a shocking blow to the Peace Corps community at large. "I am hereby terminating the contract between the Malawian Government and the United States Peace Corps. Furthermore, the Peace Corps must be completely out of the country two years from today!"

Derek sat up. "Holy crap! Judy was spot-on! The old bastard has just done more damage to the development of this country than can be imagined."

I questioned why the president would jeopardize so many thriving programs in Malawi. "What in hell are the Ministries of Health, Education and Agriculture going to do without Peace Corps Volunteers to staff so many crucial positions?"

Being masters of the obvious, we blathered on, well into the night.

Those three speeches made over three consecutive evenings spelled devastation for the Peace Corps.

There was a knock on my door at 6:00 a.m. the next morning, just as the sun was rising. Two police officers gave me ten minutes to gather my essential belongings, including my passport. They explained that the PC office would send the rest of my stuff to my home in America. They drove me to the Peace Corps office.

The staff had been alerted by Malawi government officials that the police were going to show up with me quite early. When we arrived, and after the obligatory greetings and introductions, PC Director Monroe McKay asked to have a few private moments with me. I followed him down the hall into a smaller office.

"Jack, this has turned into a monumental cluster fuck," he said with calm passion. "I haven't yet conferred with Peace Corps Headquarters in Washington, for I need to be better prepared when I do." He looked weary and understandably frazzled. "How are you holding up?"

I shook my head sadly. "I'm still in shock. Kicking me out is one thing. But the *entire* Peace Corps—that's hard for me to comprehend."

Monroe perked up. "Okay, here's the plan. I've alerted the staff that I shall be the only one to speak. Got it? We must have a united front. And please know, Jack, that we have your back. Although other PCVs have been thrown out of Malawi, this will be the first time we've ever fought back strenuously. So be patient. We're digging in for a major confrontation. Who knows—maybe we'll *all* be arrested!"

When we returned to the office, the ensuing discussion between Director McKay and the police started off calmly, yet quickly spiraled into heated, angry exchanges. Monroe began. "Thank you very much for bringing Jack here for this meeting concerning his being summarily dismissed by His Excellency Doctor Banda."

He was abruptly interrupted and corrected by the senior police officer. "By His Excellency *President* Doctor Hastings Banda, *sir!*"

"I stand duly corrected, Officer Lieutenant Maluwa," responded Monroe, pronouncing lieutenant the British way—"lef-*TEN*-ent." The director was irritated, but he kept calmly focused.

The officer explained that it was absolutely obligatory that I be required to leave Malawi that very day. That's when Monroe began to escalate.

"No way, sir! Mr. Allison is being treated unfairly, as is the Peace Corps at large, for that matter, and we shall not stand for such unwarranted, brutish behavior! I am going to contact the United States Ambassador, Mr. Jones, at eight o'clock, and we shall take emergency legal action, if necessary, if you won't compromise concerning Allison's departure."

The officer went on a long discourse that he was only following orders. He then asked if he could make a private telephone call. He and his colleague went into another office but returned quickly. No answer—too early. The discussion went on and on, back and forth, basically repeating what had already been said.

Tea, coffee and cookies (biscuits to the Brits) were served, which helped to ease the tension. After a quiet period, the officer announced, "This is indeed a rather complicated situation. Let us take our leave now. However, let's please reconvene here at 10:00 this morning."

It was only 7:20. I took a deep breath and looked around. I realized that this might very well be the last time I would ever enter the building again. The PC office was larger than most in Blantyre, yet it was still too small for the activity that went on there. Interior walls in every building in the entire country—government facilities, private homes, churches, mosques, businesses—were painted white, if they were painted. All the furnishings were basic, even pedestrian. The director's office had flags representing the United States and Malawi, and the photograph hanging on his wall was that of President Lyndon Baines Johnson. Most windows had blinds but no curtains.

There was a small crowded parking lot out back which was totally inadequate. There were only six offices in that two-story edifice, which had been poorly designed. The first floor had not been finished properly and was used only for storage. As with so many things in Malawi, the building just wasn't adequate for the demands associated with it.

When the meeting was reconvened at 10:10, Lt. Maluwa made a surprise announcement, "Ladies and gentlemen, His Excellency Minister of Finance John Tembo has insisted that Mr. McKay and Mr. Allison join him in his office at 11:00 o'clock this morning. I'm sure you know the way. Please note that one else shall be allowed to accompany them. And with that, I bid you all a good day."

We were absolutely caught off guard. A frenetic speculation began, for everyone was aware of the terrible reputation John Tembo had earned as the president's brutal enforcer. The group quietened down when I reminded them that Tembo had ended up supporting me and my musical endeavors after he had summoned me to his office eighteen months earlier. After bouncing possibilities around, including reporting this situation to *Newsweek*, *The International Herald-Tribune* and *The Times of London*, it was time for Monroe and me to drive over to Minister Tembo's office. On the way, Monroe reassured me that Peace Corps would defend me wholeheartedly.

"Minister Tembo will see you straight away," his receptionist said, smiling warmly.

John Tembo stood up and he, too, greeted us genially. After shaking hands and bidding us to be seated, he began, "Gentlemen, what has occurred is most unpleasant and disheartening. President Banda is terribly upset. I want to hear you out. Then I have some suggestions to proffer."

Obviously too early to show his hand concerning the fate of the Peace Corps, Monroe said, "Your Excellency, sir, please be aware that Jack is scheduled to leave Malawi in just a few days from now. I've brought his airline ticket with me as proof of his upcoming departure. The Peace Corps is politely adamant that he be allowed to remain in Malawi until then. Sir, we beg your indulgence. As for the Peace Corps itself, let's please save that conversation for another day."

That's when Mr. Tembo disarmed us both.

"I've had the pleasure of meeting Mr. Allison sometime back, and we enjoyed our brief session together. I have supported his work."

He and I smiled cordially at one another. Monroe was leery. Tembo continued, this time more intently, "After conferring this morning with His Excellency President Banda, we have agreed on a final proposition that, I must insist, shall not be negotiable. Jack Allison may remain in Malawi until his scheduled date of departure, if and only if the following terms are agreed to at this very moment: Allison must stay out of the public's eye. He may not interact whatsoever with the press or the radio. His activities will be monitored closely by the police. If he commits even one infraction, he shall be jailed. Do I make myself quite clear, gentlemen?"

Monroe and I were manifestly relieved. Monroe tried to engage with the Minister, yet Tembo ignored him by thanking me for my service to Malawi, wishing me all the best with my future enterprises and shaking my hand with both of his. His parting words were, "*Zikomo kwambiri, Aphiri!*" [Thank you very much, using my Malawian clan name!]

I was granted a partial reprieve. Things were to get worse for the Peace Corps.

EXPULSION AFTERMATH

"Where words fail, music speaks."

Hans Christian Anderson

After President Banda made his announcement that he had terminated the contract between the Malawian Government and the United States Peace Corps, the central office in Blantyre was on the ropes. One thing in its favor was that the wheels of bureaucracy moved slowly. What did transpire demonstrates how randomly international events occur, or at least evolve.

As the Peace Corps was winding down in Malawi, the major remaining program was education. The TB project was the first to fold, and the Malawian government was slow to follow through in arranging for those thousands of patients to receive appropriate medical follow-up, including obtaining their required medications and x-rays in a timely manner. Fortunately, our baby clinic project was taken over by Malawians who ended up being better trained than we neophyte pioneers, an exemplary reflection of the first two goals of the PC.

The program in agriculture, although quite small, was impressively successful because crucial experts had been making substantial advances   such as early computerization of applicable data and demonstration projects involving crop selection and fertilization. The rural development piece had been usurped by our public health/ environmental sanitation project, which then declined appreciably.

Secondary education was the largest, most influential facet of the Peace Corps' contribution to the development of Malawi.

Knowing this full well, and in a virtual panic about what should be done, the Minister of Education, Dr. Chilivumbu, a gentleman who had helped teach Chichewa to our group and other PC trainees, finally mustered the courage to approach the president with only six months remaining on Peace Corps' foreshortened contract. Eventually word got out about that pivotal interchange.

"Your Excellency, I am fearful that what I have to say may very well be most offensive to you, so please, sir, do not shoot the messenger. May I please continue with my report, Your Excellency?" Because his name was so long, he was fondly known as "Chili" to PCVs and staff. He was quite popular with folks "on our side of the picket fence."

The president was impatient, even gruff. "Don't waste my time with trivia! If you are here on behalf of the bloody Peace Corps, as my secretary has informed me, I do not wish to be bothered."

Minister Chilivumbu was tall and lean, and he was a grounded, solid statesmanship with an easy air of approachability. He was serious about his duties, yet had an abiding sense of self-effacing humor. Chili was respected, revered and renowned for his steadfast leadership and his ability to get disparate factions to come to consensus.

The Minister was uncommonly firm. "Your Excellency, please be apprised that Malawi desperately needs the Peace Corps to remain in our country. Please be aware that they comprise sixty percent of our secondary school teachers. To be blunt, sir, without the Peace Corps, most of our secondary schools will be forced to close."

President Banda remained silent for an uncomfortable few minutes, mulling what Minister Chilivumbu had said. Although he was sorely disappointed, the president also knew that his options were limited. Reluctantly, he said, "The Peace Corps may stay."

Chili then took advantage of this rare opening by adding, "And those Peace Corps Volunteers for health, agriculture and other specialists, I'm sure." After another long pause, Banda grunted a barely audible "Yes."

When the Peace Corps office in Blantyre received the good news, the remaining few staff members were relieved, yet they were also exhausted from what felt like battle fatigue. Although they were aware that they would not be starting from scratch, the rebuilding process would be arduous in reestablishing key contacts; sorting out specifics for housing; recruiting a full panoply of staff, including two physicians and at least one nurse; and dealing with the logistics of moving the Peace Corps office to Lilongwe, where the new capital would be located. Credible lines of communication with PC headquarters would also need to be reestablished to procure unbudgeted money for the move and to put a premium on the recruitment of staff and PCVs.

President Banda received considerable criticism from the leaders of many African countries because of his relationship with the South African government, which adhered to strict racially driven policies associated with apartheid. Banda apparently saw himself as a realist— he wanted South African financial assistance in moving the capital from Zomba in the Southern Region to Lilongwe, which was centrally located. Banda had been advised to make that strategic move to improve communication and transportation throughout the country, and soft loans from South Africa facilitated that timely transformation. The major airport was also shifted from Blantyre to Lilongwe to complete the process.

Being forced to leave Malawi was devastating for me. Peace Corps/Malawi and I were plunged into a grand funk, reeling from shared losses and disappointments. Personally, these setbacks were both monumentally mind-boggling and downright depressing. My biggest disappointment was losing the opportunity to leave the modest legacy of my educational music for the Malawian people. Had it not been for Gail's unfailing support, I might have been overcome with despair.

The obvious task at hand was figuring out what to do about being drafted. I was not avoiding the draft; rather, I thought that PC service would be a noble alternative to serving in the military. Unfortunately, I was one of many naïve Americans who wrongly thought that voluntary service with the Peace Corps somehow counted toward fulfilling a mythical guideline of not being required to perform any further service obligation. As for naivete, I was so desperate that I convinced myself that I had a chance to persuade my draft board to overturn my having been drafted. I rushed back to Florida, leaving Gail in Malawi with at least a faint hope that we could still take our elaborately planned trip home.

Things did not go well. When I appeared unannounced to the Selective Service office in Sebring, Florida, Ambrose Sturgess surprised me by agreeing to see me straight away. However, less than one minute into my plea, he interrupted me with a spitefully devilish grin on his face, "Sorry, Allison, this office doesn't deal with requests such as yours, or with *any* grievances whatsoever, for that matter."

"Excuse me, Mr. Sturgess, I am hoping to make an appeal in person to all members of the draft board. My situation is at least worthy of review, sir," I pleaded while keeping my cool. Sturgess would have none of it. He gave me a card with the name of Lt. Col. C.R. Watson, Regional Director of the Selective Service System, and ushered me out the door.

The next morning I drove the ninety miles to Ft. Pierce, a town roughly halfway down the east coast of Florida. Lt. Col. Watson saw me immediately, listened politely until I began to repeat myself, then informed me that I didn't have a snowball's chance in Hades in overturning the decision of my draft board. He did proffer a cordial suggestion, though. "Mr. Allison, I heard you mention that you're going to Denver to meet your wife's parents. By requesting in writing to your draft board that your upcoming induction be transferred there, you'll buy at least an extra month of time to spend with your wife and her family."

That afternoon I wired Gail to liquidate all our tickets, sell the car and meet me at my brother's home in Charlotte as soon as she could.

It was so good to reconnect with Gail, for both of us were drained mentally and physically. My brother, Zeb, and his wife, Sheri, were warm, gracious and hospitable, which helped ease our frustration and disappointment.

The next stop on our way to Denver was a brief trip to Florida for her to meet my parents and my six-year-old baby brother, Jeff. It was not surprising that my parents took to Gail unconditionally. However, Jeff did not. When Gail and I insisted on preparing a gourmet meal in lieu of going out to dinner (which no one could afford anyway), I was Gail's *sous chef*.

The main dish was Gail's specialty, *les oiseaux sans tete* [birds without heads]. Jeff frowned and announced, "Sure would be nice to have a hamburger!" The joyful evening was not affected by Jeff's honest, needy outburst. We four adults chuckled, and Jeff was visibly relieved when my stepfather assured him of a trip to the local hamburger joint after dessert.

Gail and I are not the only RPCVs who experienced more culture shock upon returning to the USA than when arriving in Africa. Driving on the interstate highway was particularly nerve-racking. Vehicles were so much more numerous and traveled incredibly faster. Shopping in the supermarket was overwhelming at first, with so much variety and so many choices. It was also strange not to see lots of people walking along or in the roads *everywhere*, a constant daily occurrence all over Malawi. And except for buying a car, the once obligatory art of bartering evaporated.

The two-day drive to Denver was extremely cold in our newly-acquired 1948 VW Beetle. Because the heater was not capable of keeping us even remotely warm, Gail and I layered up with extra clothing, including socks and even hats and gloves while chugging along in that little old antique. It had been ninety degrees when each of us had left Malawi, compared to minus five with the wind chill factor on our westward journey.

Gail and I had two days of "windshield time," although it was distressing not to be able to plan our future because we didn't know what the next two years would bring. The good news was that we were facing an uncertain future together. The bad news—fear of the unknown was oppressive.

INDUCTION?

"Music could ache and hurt, that beautiful music was a
place a suffering man could hide."

Pat Conroy

Once I realized that I could not fight my induction into the army, I came close to folding my tent. However, once in Denver, I decided to visit the local library of the American Friends Service. They possessed an impressive array of information related to all aspects of the Selective Service System. That's where I learned an historical issue that had most likely resulted in my being drafted. A letter to me from my draft board had been sent to my home address. The problem was that my parents had moved from Florida to Georgia for a year. Although they had obviously not received that letter, the law then was based on an "irrefutable presumption" that the letter had been received.

The more research I did at the AFS reading room, the more engaged I became in investigating my options, which including hiring an attorney. She strongly recommended that I file a *writ of habeas corpus* near the end of the upcoming induction ceremony. She explained that habeas corpus is a recourse in law which allows a person to report an unlawful detention or imprisonment to a court to determine whether the detention is lawful. But before we got that far, kismet intervened.

When I strained my back helping two guys to move a washer-dryer, I did three things: I learned the reflexes and dermatomes in my legs associated with nerve damage (this was *long* before I attended medical school); I consulted with a private physician where I performed the best under-played "John Wayne" acting job I could muster, thereby obtaining a strong letter that documented my injury; and I requested a courtesy physical exam through Denver's Selective Service System.

The local draft board approved the courtesy physical. The letter stated that I needed to report to the recruitment center located in downtown Denver at 6:00 a.m. on the day I was assigned.

The place was bedlam. In addition to hordes of young draftees, there were at least a dozen 17-year-old kids who had convinced their parents to sign for them so that they could volunteer for the army. All of us were given a folder than contained a fist full of papers, ushered to lockers, told to disrobe down to our skivvies, and then directed to follow the colored lines on the floor as directed. I was the oldest man there.

The morning dragged on. It was "hurry up and wait" time. The youngsters were quite loud and playful, snapping each other with towels, fidgeting nervously and bantering non-stop. A group of four actually made the effort to connect with me. "Hey grandpa, did you sign up, too?" teased one of the youngest.

"Yeah," I said. "Now my fantasy about getting to kill people has finally come true." The area around us suddenly got quiet for a few seconds before we all shared a hesitant laugh. Before and after that interchange I was subdued, concentrating on round two of my upcoming "John Wayne" for the examining doctor.

My name wasn't called until after 10:00 a.m. Although I had repeatedly and meticulously rehearsed my acting routine, including waddling stiffly into the exam room, the Air Force physician neither looked up as he read the letter concerning my private physical exam, nor did he ask me any questions. Instead of performing an examination on me, he abruptly stamped and signed the official forms and thrust them into my hands.

"What's all this mean, Doc?" I asked.

"Three months. You're required to report back in three months for a repeat physical. Hurry up. I have many more to see."

Friendly he was not. When I asked him who might be able to explain things to me in more detail, he brusquely referred me to a Major Nathanson on the second floor. After hurriedly (and limberly) getting dressed, I ran upstairs to find Nate Nathanson. He was friendly, even supportive.

"Mr. Allison, you've got to be the oldest one here today," he observed with an amiable grin. "I was told you have some important questions for me."

"Yes, sir. Two quick things. What does 3-Y mean, and why must I return in three months? Please don't tell me I've got to go through this all over again!"

The major took a quick look at my forms and immediately told me that I was *free.*

What? Yes, I was released from being drafted. He explained that had the physician looked closer, he would have seen my age. The 3-Y classification was a temporary status based on transient illness or injury. Since I was already twenty-six, I was no longer eligible for the draft.

I was so happy that the full force of reality took a while to seep in. Gail and I could now go on with our lives, relax, make plans, get jobs, apply for graduate school, all the while not being consumed by Uncle Sam's designs for me. Gail's parents treated us to dinner that evening at a fancy steakhouse. I managed to slosh through two martinis in celebration, yet I kept thinking about what might be in store for us.

After chilling for a few days, Gail and I started a daily exercise program. I had been drafted in mid-November, so a great deal of emotional energy had been expended over the past three months. We landed a conjoint job as cottage parents at a home for displaced children for eight girls aged seven to fifteen, sold our Beetle and bought a low-mileage used MGB-GT. While still in Malawi the prior year we had taken the Graduate Record Examination and had applied for masters programs at the UNC School of Public Health—now the UNC Gillings School of Global Public Health—in Chapel Hill.

Working with the kids at the Colorado Christian Home was phenomenal. The girls responded beautifully to our "parenting," for they were starved for affection, discipline and direction. Gail and I took the job seriously, and we received frequent encouraging feedback from the director and the two social workers. We also loved our schedule—on for four days and nights, and off for the other three. We showed up for all the events and activities involving the girls at school, helped them with their homework in the evenings, read to them before they said their prayers each night, and were intimately involved with their playtime after school and on weekends.

Then fate intervened yet again. Gail received her acceptance to the MPH program in Maternal and Child Health three days before I got mine in Community Mental Health. The bonus was that I received a tax-free fellowship worth $20,000 in today's money. Since classes were to begin in late August, we worked at the home for six-and-a-half months.

Saying goodbye to the girls was extremely difficult.

CADENZA

"Music is the divine way to tell beautiful, poetic things to the heart."

— Pablo Casals

Toward the end of my senior year in high school, I began to fantasize about my future career. Becoming a music teacher was one option, although intuitively—before the introduction of the "10,000-hours rule" on how to be successful—I knew that I had not yet spent the necessary time or had the motivation to perfect the baritone and to learn basic music theory.

One afternoon after class, I perused some folders in the career counselor's office. An article that impressed me was by an aging family physician who waxed on about his most satisfying career in medicine. Late that afternoon driving home I decided to stop by a local family physician's office. The door was open.

"Hello! May I come in?" I shouted.

Dr. Osterling was catching up on patients' charts. "Come on in. What may I do for you?"

"Doc, I'm wondering what my major in college should be if I want to become a physician."

Dr. Osterling offered me a seat. "Well, you've come to the right place. I did something similar when I was your age, and the advice I got was most helpful."

Although I asked only two questions, Dr. Osterling calmly laid out in succinct detail what possible majors to consider, how important grades were, how rewarding being a physician was, and what long hours he worked—leaving less time for his wife, children, parents and in-laws. After allowing me to fill him in on my grades and activities, he encouraged me to "press on" with pursuing my dream, if that's what I eventually decided. Dr. Osterling was patient with me, and he treated me as an adult.

Once I got to Warren Wilson College, then a junior college and now one of seven work-study colleges in America, I became a pre-med major with an A- average. I struggled to make Cs in algebra.

As an undergraduate at UNC-Chapel Hill, I had majored in chemistry, yet obtained a Bachelor of Arts instead of a Bachelor of Science. I just could not do the requisite calculus for a BS degree.

My deficient math skills were evident when I took the Medical College Admissions Test (MCAT)—I scored in the lower 3rd percentile in math, which caused me to panic! I made an appointment with the Director of Admissions at the UNC School of Medicine.

"Dr. Straughn, considering my dismally low score in math on the MCAT, what are my options? Do I need to repeat the MCAT, sir?" I asked.

He took his time responding as he deliberately thumbed through my application file. He volunteered that my interviews for medical school had gone well.

"I note that you're pursing a master's in public health degree across the street, correct?"

When I answered affirmatively to his question, he said, "Then you must take a required course in biostatistics. Have you done so yet?"

"I'm taking it this semester."

He paused briefly. "Okay, Mr. Allison. I'll make a deal with you. If you earn an A or honors in biostat, I can guarantee that you'll be accepted to medical school here. Otherwise, I just can't be sure. Any further questions?"

I was taken aback yet encouraged by his direct offer. Dr. Straughn was not a physician. He had earned a Ph.D. in Medical Technology. He had also garnered a solid reputation of being tough, yet fair.

It still amazes me how this all played out. I had become friendly with Dr. Straughn's secretary, a very bright and attractive African American young woman named Beverly. Since she was fascinated with my Peace Corps experience in Africa, she always asked me to share a story or two whenever I dropped by with a question or minor request. When I did so in mid-December, right before Christmas break, she smiled jovially as I approached her desk.

"Good afternoon, Mr. Allison. How may I help you this fine day?" Her demeanor was definitely more animated than ever before.

"Yes, please. I have heard from some of my friends that they have been notified of their acceptance to med school here. May I ask if Dr. Straughn has sent me a letter?"

"You know, Mr. Allison, that I am not at liberty to share that information with you," she said with a hint of pseudo-disapproval. I didn't say anything for a few moments. Something in her gleaming dark brown eyes told me that there was possibly good news in them.

"What I can share with you, Mr. Allison, is that I posted a letter to you from Dr. Straughn two days ago. That's all I'm allowed to say, if I haven't said too much already. Please go home and check your mailbox!"

Although I was encouraged by our interchange, I still did not know Dr. Straughn's verdict. I raced home to Bynum, a tiny unincorporated community south of Chapel Hill where Gail and I lived. I was crestfallen when I opened our mailbox and found no letter from the Admissions Office.

The next afternoon was even worse. Still no letter. Gail and I had delayed leaving town on our vacation to spend Christmas with Gail's family in Denver because we were so anxious to receive the news, good or bad.

I called Beverly. When I explained what had transpired—and before I could beg her to please tell me what was in the letter—she politely cut me off. "Jack, you've been accepted into medical school here. Please, please do not tell *anyone* that I told you!"

"Beverly, are you sure? My wife and I—"

She cut me off again. "Jack, I typed the letter. Relax! You're in!"

I was awash with feelings of ecstasy to Zen-like calm to satisfying relief to hopeful anticipation—from the cacophony of despair to the polyphony of bliss. What was so unbelievable was that I had been accepted into medical school *before* I had even taken our semester's final exams within the UNC School of Public Health! I promptly became determined to honor Dr. Straughn's bargain with me, and my motivation became quite intense over the holiday break and the run-up to finals. I studied biostatistics day and night, and I ended up earning an honors grade. That was truly an accomplishment for me!

The next week, however, I was not able to distinguish the differences among the mean, the mode, and the median.

IT HAD TAKEN TEN YEARS FROM my high school dream of becoming a physician to finally being accepted to medical school. It was a marvelous journey which had included a junior college, a university and a school of public health, interspersed with a most meaningful three-year tour in Malawi, Central Africa, as a U.S. Peace Corps Volunteer.

I had joined the Peace Corps to allow me the time to sort out whether to pursue a career in medicine or the ministry. My experience in Africa was invaluable in getting me focused on medicine. Being a Peace Corps Volunteer solidified my desire to live a life of service because those three years were truly transformative.

Medical school was pivotal in determining the trajectory of the rest of my career and personal life. Although I had thought I was destined to be a family physician, armed with a broad perspective on patient care and long-term relationships with patients, my personality just wasn't suited for those admirable intentions. I needed more "juice."

I came to realize that I'm a "stress junky"—not knowing what emergency patient may be coming through the door was exhilarating to me—and being challenged to be prepared for the unknown was something I truly relished.

And, I learned in Malawi that I loved to teach. That carried over in both medicine and public health. I chose academic emergency medicine as my vocation, allowing the substrate of music to bubble forth consistently as my avocation, especially in the realm of public health.

I continue to value and appreciate the balance between immediate, curative, and acute care medicine and the patient, prolonged, wider scope of preventive medicine—on both continents.

In June 2005, I was asked by the U.S. State Department to tour the entire country of Malawi to sing and speak about AIDS awareness, education, and prevention.

Below, Malawian women do an interpretive dance about AIDS prevention.

AFRICA REVISITED

"Music, when soft voices die, vibrates in the memory."

Percy Bysshe Shelley

After leaving Malawi in mid-December 1969, I would not return for another twenty-five years. Gail and I had amicably parted ways and I had become remarried—to the love of my life, Sue Wilson.

Since then I've been back to Africa many times. In 1982, I was awarded a USAID contract to teach public health engineering students how to best introduce ventilated improved pit (VIP) latrines in the peri-urban areas of Dar es Salaam, Tanzania. My wife, Sue, who was five months pregnant with our son, Josh, joined me on that mission.

We used dark brown sock puppets–Mary the Mosquito and Fred the Fly—plus a catchy jingle to "complain" that their "neighborhood" had been ruined by the new latrines: no odor, along with no mosquitoes, flies, roaches and rats. The students and faculty were most appreciative of our simple, light-hearted approach to health education, again geared for the masses.

Although I had received numerous calls from Malawians who had traveled to the U.S.A., our answering machine was blinking when our family returned from a trip to the beach. Those calls were from Malawi.

"Jack, this is Ted Sneed. Remember me? I was a PCV teacher stationed north of you in Ntcheu. We need you to come back to Malawi to help with the AIDS crisis. Please write songs for our HIV-AIDS campaign! I'll leave my number."

I had not expected such a warm invitation. I played the next message.

"Aphiri, Junius Chirwa here. I was in primary school when you were a Peace Corps Volunteer. People here remember you and they remember your music. We hope you will consider returning to Malawi as soon as possible to write and sing some songs about combating HIV-AIDS. Please call back soon."

Still amazed, I played the third message.

"Jack, hi, I'm Loreen Pulaski, Director of Project HOPE in Malawi. Ted and Junius are working with me. Your name keeps coming up as we discuss ways of stemming the HIV-AIDS epidemic which is spreading rapidly throughout Malawi. Your musical approach would be most helpful. Please call me back at your earliest convenience."

I had just begun a sabbatical year as Sterling Distinguished Professor and Chair of the Department of Emergency Medicine at the Brody School of Medicine, East Carolina University, in Greenville, North Carolina. Since I was now afforded the time, I was tremendously excited about signing on with the proposal.

The invitation was made in mid-July 1994, and with all the bureaucratic machinations necessary to make the one-month trip, I arrived in Malawi three months later.

When I stepped off in the plane in Lilongwe, I was ushered immediately into an area set up for the local and national press for me to deliver a press conference. The rapid-fire questions were not what I had expected, for twenty-five years earlier the press had been tightly controlled by the government.

"Jack, what does it feel like to be back in Malawi after being declared *persona non grata* by former President Hastings Banda and summarily forced to leave this country?" "Do you harbor any ill will toward him?" "Why have you returned after such a long time?" "What do you hope to accomplish?" Will there be any new music in the offing?" "Do you feel welcomed now?" And all of that was within the first fifteen seconds!

In spite of jet lag, I managed to remain calm and answer every question with as much poise as I could muster. I graciously thanked the dozen reporters for their interest in our work. I assured them that it was wonderful to be back; told them that the distant past had no bearing on our present efforts to join the fight against HIV-AIDS; and said that we would keep them apprised of our progress over the next four weeks.

What amazed me is that I ended up speaking at least one-fourth of the press conference in Chichewa, using key words and phrases to emphasize and bolster my responses. I had not spoken their national language in twenty-five years. It was obviously in my marrow.

In my contract with Project HOPE, I was asked to write, produce and record three songs about AIDS. Since I had already written three songs before I'd left the USA, I wrote three more within the next two days. Then I went about auditioning eight of the most popular bands in the Blantyre area, which was no easy task. Most of that had to occur at night when each band was performing at a local hot spot around the city. I ended up choosing the two best and divided my six songs evenly between them. Next came rehearsal time and then auditioning a plethora of other acts that would become part of the official launch of our AIDS program—awareness, education and prevention.

Daily rehearsals were long and exhausting, and the logistics of getting two bands together on "African time" were frustratingly inefficient. We finally spent two half-days at MBC, recording three songs with each band. Interestingly, the Siemans reel-to-reel recording equipment (originally from West Germany) used for our recordings was the very same that had been used to record my sixteen songs and jingles twenty-five years prior.

Before the songs could be played on MBC or any other radio station, per the customary protocol, there had to be an official launch of the project. That occurred on a Friday night at the posh Mt. Soche Hotel in downtown Blantyre. Although I knew that a governmental representative would be required to conduct the launch, I was blown away when in walked the Minister of Sport and Culture, the Hon. Dr. Chilibvumbu! He and I hugged and reminisced before the festivities began with opening remarks by Chili. After the greetings, thanks yous and acknowledgments, he began:

"Ladies and gentlemen, I have known Dr. Jack Allison since December of 1966. However, we did not meet in one of the big cities in America—not in New York, or Chicago, or Los Angeles. No. We spent a month together in the rainforest above Arecibo, Puerto Rico, where I taught Jack how to speak Chichewa. Add I must add that I did a magnificent job, did I not?"

The room rocked with applause and laughter, for Chili was still as popular as ever with the Malawian populace. He had set the table nicely for us that evening, and the opening concert was a tremendous success. And because the other acts were also so well received—a dance troupe, two short mini-plays, a chorus, and a poet—what precipitated afterward was a national songwriting contest for *Songs About AIDS*. Along with my six songs, the project was overwhelmingly successful.

Early one evening in the autumn of 2004, I received a call from a woman in the U.S. State Department as Sue and I were preparing dinner together. She reminded me that the AIDS epidemic in Malawi was still a major public health issue. She stressed that what was needed was for me to return to Malawi to tour the country to speak and sing about AIDS awareness, education and prevention.

"Lady, I seriously doubt if Malawians will be eager to listen to a sixty-year-old dude. I'm not twenty-five anymore."

"On the contrary, Dr. Allison," she said, "your name keeps coming up in conversations about how best to attack the ongoing HIV-AIDS epidemic in Malawi. You will be heartened by both the reception and the response you will receive, sir."

We then lapsed into a negotiation. She wanted me to tour Malawi from immediately after Thanksgiving until right before Christmas. I agreed to go after our son Josh had graduated as an undergraduate from UNC-Chapel Hill, which would entail the month of June. She accepted my counter offer.

The 2005 tour of Malawi went swimmingly. After Josh and I had been in country for three days, we were joined by Sue and Josh's girlfriend at the time. Before their arrival, Josh and I had been busy auditioning bands for the tour. We chose the National Health Education Band, the best of the lot.

And was I ever wrong about my reservations of whether my performances would be well received! Pre-concert publicity by the Department of State had been handled quite well—3,000 people attended each daytime concert, usually held on a local soccer pitch, and 50-100 people showed up each evening for my verbal presentations, which were augmented with two or three of my AIDS songs. I was especially heartened by the question-and-answer sessions, for the young attendees asked cogent, pertinent, penetrating questions. Josh was my roadie, a role he relished.

One early suggestion from State was that I audition other performers to enhance each concert. At each venue, I screened an incredible number of interested parties—including a one-man band, choruses, church choirs, dance troupes, poets, and casts of miniplays. Truth be known, I did not eliminate anyone or any group that auditioned, for the amalgamated and enthusiastic talent was impressive.

Each performance lasted three hours, and the crowds were attentive, responsive and well-mannered.

Because the custom in Malawi is for an official event to be opened by a government representative, the Minister of Sport and Culture, the Hon. Lindani Chimpando, gave a speech—first in English, then in Chichewa—before we kicked off the inaugural concert. After the usual warm, welcoming greetings to everyone, she then added, "When I was but a little girl, an eleven-year-old in standard six, Jack Allison came to my school and gave an educational presentation. Before he left our classroom, he sang a song for us."

She then sang *Ufa wa Mtedza* in its entirety! All of us in our group of four had to fight back tears of wonderment, knowing full well that since my songs had been banned, she had memorized *Ufa* over thirty-five years ago.

Furthermore, all of my performances were totally in Chichewa. Josh used his favorite phrase when he mentioned, "Dad, I thought you were blowing smoke up my ass when you told me you could speak the language." Sue was similarly impressed, although she referred to a different anatomical part (her nose).

OUR DAUGHTER, ADRIENNE, HAD MISSED THE tour of Malawi in 2005 because she was studying for the bar exam, so Sue and I decided to take her and her husband, Bob, to Malawi for a one-month private tour of the country. It's the only time I've ever been to Africa when I didn't have to work.

As a little girl, Adrienne was amazingly articulate, using three and four syllable words at an early age. She also started reading before she turned four. Adrienne has always been "an old soul" in the most positive sense. She's been a marvelous big sister to Josh, often defending him against neighborhood and schoolyard bullies. She was an elegant, graceful dancer, and she was involved in a panoply of school activities. Adrienne was president of her senior class, and she had leading roles in two plays.

After high school, Adrienne attended UNC-Chapel Hill, double-majoring in English and Women's Studies. She took advantage of a semester abroad at the University of Sussex in England. She went on to law school at UNC. Out of a class of two hundred and thirty-five, she was one of eight inducted into the prestigious Davis Society. Sue and I could not have been more proud of her.

The four of us had a marvelous time together, including visits to Nsiyaludzu Village and with Achitowe and his family near Monkey Bay. They were impressed with the warmth of the Malawian people— and the prevalent poverty throughout the country. Adrienne and Bob climbed Mt. Mulanje in one day, Malawi's highest peak, at 10,000 feet. I had done so in 1968.

While staying at the chic Club Makokola Resort on beautiful Lake Malawi, something unexpected happened. After breakfast, as the four of us were walking down to the beach, shouts in English rang out from three Malawian kayakers, "Aphiri, where's Joshua?"

Adrienne particularly was undone. "Dad, you and Josh were here three years ago! How's this possible?"

I explained that the kayakers were curio hawkers from a nearby village. Josh had readily taken to bartering. And because he and the peddlers were close in age, they had ended up spending extra time together.

I spent the month of February 2012 with Medical Teams International in Kenya and Somalia, where I provided emergency care to Somali refugees who were suffering from a terrible drought. I also spent approximately ten percent of my time using puppets to teach Somalis about VIP latrines and tippy-taps for protecting water for hand washing thereafter. This involvement brought back fond memories of the USAID 1982 trip to Dar es Salaam with Sue.

In October 2012, I visited with Achitowe for four nights before I reported to neighboring Zambia for a three-week voluntary public health assignment with Marion Medical Mission. I helped install 112 shallow water wells, which was grueling, gratifying work. I also got to use my Chichewa totally during that mission.

I spent a week in Achitowe's compound in April 2016 after having spent a week in Cape Town, South Africa, where I was honored for being the first president of the International Federation for Emergency Medicine. It was IFEM's silver jubilee. I didn't use any notes during my ten-minute speech, interjecting light humor into my historical oration. At the conclusion, I raised my wine glass and sang an *a capella* toast, *Down Among the Dead Men,* to the assemblage of international emergency physician delegates. I received a prolonged, enthusiastic standing ovation.

In July of both 2017 and 2018, I spent two-and-a-half weeks each year as senior consultant with the Fulbright Association's WASH project in Malawi. Our ongoing goal is to improve water, sanitation, health and hygiene in two model villages. Our team has planted 2,000 trees with Malawian villagers, and we have introduced VIP latrines and protected water supplies.

The most challenging part of our project is the hygiene facet. Only five percent of secondary school girls graduate. When girls have their monthly period, they miss a week of schooling because they don't have access to sanitary products. Additionally, tampons are disallowed culturally.

The good news is that my involvement with the Fulbright Association has rekindled my creative juices: I have written and recorded another dozen songs and jingles for our project, including *Deforestation, Girls Not Brides*, and *Malawi Children's Village.*

The first line of *Deforestation* is: "What shall we do when we cut down the last tree?"

Josh and me climbing Mt. Kilimanjaro in 2005

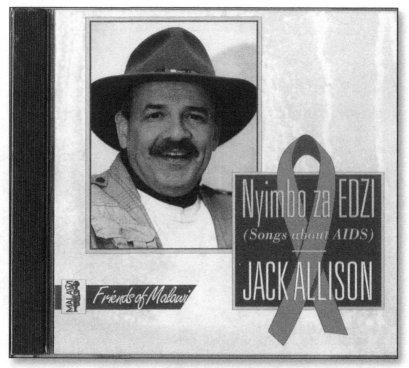

CD produced at MBC (Malawi Broadcasting Corporation), 1994

Postlude

CURRENTLY, MORE THAN 130 PEACE CORPS Volunteers are serving throughout Malawi (7,300 worldwide) in program areas of education, health and environment. At the time of this writing, all have been withdrawn from service because of the COVID-19 pandemic.

More than three thousand PCVs have served in The Warm Heart of Africa since 1964, but the future of the Peace Corps worldwide may be in jeopardy given the current political climate in Washington, D.C.

Serving in the U.S. Peace Corps was a life-changer for me, as most eturned Peace Corps Volunteers would agree concerning their own experiences. We end up receiving far more than we give, but not by our choice. That's an observation of the existential calculus of the universe that determines how things work out.

Being forced to leave Malawi was quite emotional for me. My feelings were intensified not only by having been drafted into the army after having already served my country for three years, but also because I was kicked out for such unwarranted, cruel pettiness. Those two heavy body blows painfully added to my own sadness of having to say goodbye to so many dear friends, neighbors and colleagues. Malawi had become my second home.

Looking back, there were parallels with what Peace Corps/Malawi and I faced. We had to build and rebuild while not having to start from scratch. We healed through mourning our losses, yet after a modicum of time we resurfaced—stronger mentally and emotionally from that transient trauma.

Three years in Africa taught me that the major pressure to facilitate change is *time* and that change doesn't come easy, no matter where one lives in the world. Most PVCs serve for two years—I was extremely fortunate to have been granted a third year—yet no matter how the pie chart is sliced, it takes time for community development to evolve and take root. That's why it's so essential to have a replacement volunteer or host country national to carry on with unfinished projects.

Life ain't easy anywhere one lives—some places are tougher than others. Calloused Westerners are wont to say that life in Malawi is cheap. I observed that life is precious there and that it is more threatened, more vulnerable, more fragile by lack of sufficient education, by pervasive poverty, and by the prevalence of so many health challenges—the familiar triad of ignorance, poverty and disease.

People from different cultures have in common more shared positive characteristics, needs, wants and dreams than we tend to appreciate. That global realization becomes manifest when we have the opportunity to live and work together toward shared goals. Patience, along with an abiding acceptance of one another's differences, are the essential keys to fostering peace and understanding.

I shall be eternally grateful for what medicine, music and public health have meant to me over the years. That trilogy has caused my cup to run over with gratitude, enhanced with an ingrained and profound happiness.

Amen.

Acknowledgments

Writing my memoir would not have been possible without the patient, superb guidance of Victoria Fann, writing coach extraordinaire, who helped me transform my writing from the foundation of medical scientific research to what you are now holding in your hand.

Thanks to Vally Sharpe, the consummate professional in layout, design, book cover and photograph machinations.

Thanks to my editorial assistants — Adrienne, Allison, Sue Wilson, John Lambert, John Hutcheson, and Jim Dedman — for their meticulous attention to detail.

Thanks to Marian Beil of Peace Corps Writers and John Coyne of Peace Corps Worldwide.

Thanks to my partner in music, Jim Hunt.

Thanks to members of Malawi XI, XIV and IV for their ongoing, palpable support, especially Gail Allison, Bill Schmidt, Cissy Woomer Ellis, Gordon Radley, Mark Robbins, Lee Ellison, Tom Powers, George Little, Roger Hofmeister, June Fulbright, Marty Bibel, Art Weinstein, Kevin Denny, and Tom & Ruth Nighswander.

And to members of three groups that continue to perform laudable, unselfish work in Malawi: Friends of Malawi, Malawi Childrens' Village, and Together! ACT Now.

About the Author

Dr. Jack Allison served as a Peace Corps Volunteer in Malawi, Africa, 1967-69. His public health education was punctuated by many original songs & jingles which became quite popular with Malawians throughout the country.

Jack has had a distinguished career in academic emergency medicine, with an emphasis on public health. He responded to the earthquake in Haiti in January 2010 by treating hundreds of quake victims. In February 2012 he volunteered in Kenya and Somalia where he provided both emergency care and public health education to hundreds of Somali refugees; then in October, he volunteered in Zambia where he helped to install 112 shallow water wells. Since 2017 Jack has been a senior consultant to the Fulbright Association's WASH project in Malawi.

Allison's avocation is singing/songwriting. He has written over 120 songs & jingles and recorded over 100 of those. Since 1967, he has raised $160,000 with his music, and he & his wife, Sue Wilson, have given away all of those monies to various charitable organizations, including $30,000 to help feed Malawian children who have been orphaned because their parents have died of AIDS.

Made in the USA
Middletown, DE
20 June 2020